A SHOT IN THE DARK

D1614405

A SHOT IN THE DARK

a day in the night of a
new york city bartender

BARRY REEVES

BRYCE
CULLEN
PUBLISHING

BRYCE
CULLEN
PUBLISHING

PO Box 731
Alpine, NJ 07620
brycecullen.com

ISBN 978-1-935752-37-0

Library of Congress Control Number: 2013935358

Printed in the United States of America

10 9 8 7 6 5 4 3 2 1

Thanks to my parents, Dolores and Tom,
for being Catholic and not using birth control.

INTRODUCTION

This story is true. Of course, there may be some lies, and some of it did not happen, but it's all true. As my mother would say, "Never let the truth get in the way of a good story." There might even be a joke or two thrown in for good measure. At the end of the day or night for me, if I think it's funny and it makes me laugh, I will write about it. So please don't get upset—it's only a joke.

As a bartender it's always good to have a wee joke or funny story to tell your customers—so here we go. By the way, many of the names in these stories have been changed in order to protect the guilty!

This book started out as a series of letters, and now emails, back home to my mate "Smithy" in Ireland. It's about my time working behind a bar on the West Side of Manhattan, New York City, for over ten years. Hell's Kitchen, as it is more commonly known. To all the great people, friends, and drunks I have met, I thank you. All the police officers, firemen, gangsters, priests, hookers, pimps, professors, lawyers, transvestites, celebrities, wankers, and so on, I thank you for all the stories.

Growing up in Ireland, everybody seems to have a story or line—some with good intentions, some not, but mostly good, I think. Ireland, for the most part, is a simple, plain world. That is probably why some of the greatest writers in the world hail from Ireland—Joyce, Wilde, Becket, and Behan, just to name a few. You need an imagination to survive.

Regardless of how much money you have in your bank account or how important you think you are, the most valuable tool you will ever have is your imagination.

The first time I ever saw America, and particularly NYC, on TV, I knew I wanted to be a part of it. All the lights and sounds really excited and impressed me. The different-looking people. The people with the nice teeth. It wasn't like the plain gray world that I was used to—Dublin. So from those early days I made a conscious effort to get to America. I always loved to travel, and

I thought, once I got to America the rest of the world would be there for the taking.

Everyone's life, including yours and mine, reflects a moment in time—your very own unique footprint in the sand. Everyone's life is a story. This one's mine. I hope you like it.

So please, sit back and relax, turn off your TV, and turn on your imagination—you're gonna need it. And remember to always tip your bartender.

Summer 1999

Well, Smithy, where do I start? I arrived at the Port Authority Bus Station from John F. Kennedy Airport safe and sound. What a sight to see for the first time—the New York City skyline. We have all seen it many times on TV, but until you see it in person you really can't imagine the absolute beauty of it all. The fantastic hoorair of New York City. It's mesmerizing.

All I have is an address to meet Mick on the west side of Manhattan—Ninth Avenue and Thirty-Fourth Street. I walk outside of the bus station on Forty-Second Street and Eighth Avenue, and I'm overrun with people. The last time I have seen this many people in one place—actually, I've never seen this many people in one place before. The streets dance up and down, up and down. What amazes me is how it is so well organized. It just seems to flow naturally—like a river, a fast-flowing river of people. People walking in all directions, and yet it just works.

I walk up to this friendly-looking man, and I ask him where the address is that's written on my piece of paper. I say, "Excuse me, mister, do you know how to get to Ninth Avenue and Thirty-Fourth Street?" He looks at me, straight in the face, as he continues to walk, smiles, and says, "Go fuck yourself." *Wow*, I think to myself, *hmmm, interesting*. It was at that very moment, Smithy, that exact point, that I knew I was in my town, and this was the place and city for me. I thank the kind gentleman and go on my way.

What he didn't realize was that saying, "Go fuck yourself" to an Irishman is the same as saying, "Welcome!"

I come from a place that swears. I feel at home swearing. I've cursed my whole life, as we all have, Smithy. Right? I think it's a rather useful language, to be honest with ya. The man at the bus station told me to go "fuck myself," as he put it. Totally made me feel at home, and I also knew that our conversation was over. *Perfect*, as I see it. People say swearing is a limited vocabulary. I disagree. It's a get-to-the-point vocabulary. Fuck that, I know at least 123 words and I still prefer *fuck*. Or my favorite, *ya fucker*. I've yet to find the equivalent to "fuck off." It's final. When you hear "fuck off," you know exactly where you stand. There's no misunderstanding.

Anyway, I continue rambling down Eighth Avenue, in awe of what is unfolding around me but a wee bit anxious, too. I am looking at all the different faces, hearing the many accents and the unique sounds and smells of the city. When my breath starts to return slightly, I can smell the overwhelming aroma of piss on every corner and the smell of diesel fuel from the bus exhausts. It's quite an interesting combination that seems to follow you no matter where you go. It's kinda sweet, actually. I notice as I continue down the street, these people, preachers I assume. Standing on the street corners, holding large crosses, and saying, "The Lord will return and we will all answer for the pain and suffering we have caused!" ("Speak for yourself, mate," I say under my breath.) I can't help but laugh to myself. I'm thinking, *If the Lord does happen to return, a cross is probably the last thing he ever wants to see. That's kinda rubbing it in, wouldn't you say? It would be almost like buying a cripple a bike for Christmas.*

I voice my concerns to these very friendly New Yorkers, and again I get a very encouraging, welcoming response—at least they're consistent.

Another thing I notice about New York are all the colors—so many different colors. The vibrancy and color of the city is very different from where we grew up, Smithy. Gray is the most popular color in Dublin. *Damp* is a color in Dublin.

Finally, I arrive at the address to meet our friend Mick from back home. Sure enough, it's a bar, and thank God for that, as I'm dying for a beer after my long journey. Not so much the flight over but rather the journey down Eighth Avenue. Mick is waiting for me with two pints of Guinness. He's a good fuckin' man—top drawer. As it turns out, the bar where I'm meeting him, he works there, too. He tells me they are looking for some help. To make a long story painful, Smithy, I start this Friday night. My shifts behind the bar will be every Friday night, all day Saturday, and Sunday—for brunch? I asked Mick for any advice ahead of my first night behind the bar. He says, "Don't fuck the waitresses."

Cheers for now, mate. I will let you know how I get on.

Saturday, June 5, 1999
My First Night

I started work last night at 6 p.m. I was a wee bit nervous, but at the same time very eager and extremely excited to get my life started in New York City. It's been a whirlwind few days. I got a shoebox apartment on Ninth Avenue, just up the street from the bar. That helps if only to keep my stuff. Don't think I will spend much time in it.

Mick introduced me to a lad called Randy who was looking for a room-mate. He comes into the bar and is a friend of Mick's. (I giggle when I hear his name.)

He asks me what I'm laughing at. "So your name is Horny, is that what you're telling me?" I say.

"What?" Randy says with a puzzled look on his face.

"Your parents named you Horny. Excellent, I like it. Wish I had a cool name like that."

Anyway, we arranged to meet outside this apartment block on Ninth Avenue and Thirty-Fifth Street, to look at his apartment. I say to Randy that the apartment is very small. He says, "Shut up, you're still in the elevator." He eventually shows me the apartment and the bedroom I will call home for now—I prefer the elevator. It will barely fit a bed, but I will figure it out. The walls are crooked and the floors uneven. It was like the last ten minutes of *Titanic*. "If I ever have a daughter, I'm going to have to call her Eileen," I say to Randy. I think he's starting to appreciate the Irish sense of humor as he laughs and explains that all NYC apartments are like this. "The trick is to come home drunk every night." I think Randy and I will get on just fine.

He goes on to tell me there's a "Murphy bed" in the wall.

"Now, Randy, you are taking the piss. I know I'm Irish, but Murphy bed? Come on."

"Pull on this," he says, and I am already thinking he's pulling my leg. Sure enough, this bed comes out of the wall. Fuck, the Yanks think of everything. Only in America—a bed in a wall! No wonder they were first on the moon.

There are red marks on the walls—where somebody tried to swing a cat! It's okay for now, I suppose. I'm really just happy to find a place so quickly and so convenient to my job.

My first night in the apartment, Randy asks me if I fancy splitting a pie. Not to be rude, I say, "Why not?" assuming it's some kind of pastry with apples or strawberries in it. I don't really have a sweet tooth, but right now I'm just trying to fit in. You shoulda seen the surprise I got when a large pizza pie showed up. What a pleasant surprise—better than what I was expecting. Well, Smithy, 456 Ninth Avenue, Apartment 3C, will be my new home for the unforeseeable future.

Sorry for the rant, but you know what I'm like at times.

So I walk into the bar, and it's packed, and Mick is already running around the bar. He says, "Just jump in and start taking orders"—no settling in, just thrown right in. Holy shit, for fuck's sake!

I manage to get through the night—I think. My feet are fuckin' killing me, and I'm thinking that I would be told not to come back. That would be my first and last night working behind a New York City bar. Mick gives me almost three hundred dollars (thinking that now he would tell me it's not going to work out), hands me the keys and the code to the alarm, and tells me to open up at nine o'clock tomorrow morning. "Okay?" he says.

"Sure, no problem, thanks," I say as I head out the door, not really sure what I'm saying or agreeing to.

I'm walking up the street to my new apartment listening to all the jingles of the city; it's like an orchestra. All the people still out at four thirty in the morning, the city very much wide awake and alive. It's true what they say: this city never sleeps. I can't believe what just happened—I'm buzzing. It was such a surreal experience, and a moment I believe will stay with me for a very long time.

Saturday morning comes way too quickly, considering I could not sleep a wink because of my racing mind, thinking about my friends and family back in Ireland. The content noise of rubbish trucks, fire engines, and police cars whizzing by my bedroom window, and of course . . . my pounding sore feet.

As I'm walking the few blocks to the bar the next morning, getting closer, I notice a bunch of folks waiting outside the bar. One says to me, "Are you the new bartender? Well, hurry the fuck up and open the bar. I need a drink." I think it's the same fella I asked for directions when I first arrived. I tell you one thing, Smithy, they're pretty eager over here in America. The bar is on Ninth Avenue between Thirty-Third and Thirty-Fourth Street. At either end of the block is a diner. On Thirty-Third Street you have the Cheyenne Diner, which is an "old school" diner, or so the locals say. It's been there since the thirties and looks and tastes like it. On Thirty-Fourth you have the Skylight Diner, which is the better one; however, both are owned by the same person—George the Greek. On one side of the bar you have a Chinese restaurant, a jewelry store, a hardware store, and a couple of apartment buildings. On the other side you have a shoe repair store, a photo shop, another Chinese restaurant, and a donut shop. I met Steve, who works in the twenty-four-hour donut shop, last night. He seems very nice and welcomed me into the neighborhood, tossing a few extra donuts into my bag. The diners are open twenty-four hours on either corner, but I was surprised to see a coffee and donut shop open around the clock. He explained that the Midtown South Police Station is across the street, and as he put it, "They love their coffee and donuts." So much for all those stereotypes, hey, Smithy?

This seems to be your typical layout for a city block on the West Side of Manhattan. Across the street is the YMCA (or for the dyslexic, Macy's), which seems to be very popular, as I've already met a lot of the residents from there. I will show you it all when you come over. Talk to you soon, mate.

TWO

Monday, October 18, 1999
My First Few Months in New York City!

When I think of my first few months in New York City, Smithy, many mixed emotions come running through my mind. The excitement of first stepping foot on the island of Manhattan. The nights in my wee apartment lying on the floor listening to the muffled creaking of the floorboards above me. My crooked bedroom. The constant traffic whizzing by the apartment. The rubbish trucks and police cars that seem to show up just as you're about to nod off—taunting you almost. The parking lot across the street that has that fuckin' annoying white light that never goes out—ever. Mind you, it's handy in the morning as it also shows the time and temperature. Helps me decide what to wear. Thinking about my family and friends back home in Dublin and worrying if I can make it here. But, most importantly, Smithy, how much I love this place. Happy to be under the flannel sheets and thick comforter, warm and dry. Loving this town. Where else would you get such an encouraging welcome?

Mind you, people are very aggressive here. "What the fuck do you want?" "Sorry," I say, "I'm just looking for the shops . . . lady." That's what happened last night on my way home.

Like I said, everybody has beautiful, white teeth here. Just like you see in the movies. Maybe it's because everyone is chewing gum. This fella asked me if I wanted some gum. I'm like, "No thanks, my mother always told me not to accept anything from strangers." There must be something to it; I've made it this far. I'm in bloody NYC.

Anyway, he says, "When the flavor is gone, I just throw it away." In Ireland, as you know, Smithy, when the flavor is gone—dinner's ready.

They all wear hats. What's with the baseball hats? I think Americans wear hats because they don't want to be recognized. That's why they're all bald. You need to let the sun in.

Somebody gave me the finger today in New York City. Can you believe it?—in New York.

Smithy, working behind the bar is hard work but great craic. Funny, I said that the other night and somebody thought I wanted crack. As you know, when we say "great craic," we mean great fun. Now come on, I would never do a drug named after a part of my body. I was actually dating a heroin addict for a while. She had a lot of love to give, but it was all in vein.

It's strange, there is an air of safety working behind the bar that I don't feel elsewhere. I feel safe generally, and I love the hustle and bustle of the NYC streets, but there's just something about being behind the bar. My shield. That maybe three-foot-wide slab of mahogany. It's my little space that no one else is allowed to enter. By invitation only. Maybe because of living in this busy, overcrowded city it's the one place that I can control and actually be truly alone and untouched. I know it might sound strange, but it feels good to me.

Brunch is very popular here. America is great at coming up with names. Nobody beats America, particularly in marketing. Brunch—very clever. Another reason to eat. Genius.

Well, I'm making Bloody Marys to beat the band. Bloody Mary after Bloody Mary, as I'm working brunch on the weekends. I'm bleedin' sick of making them, to be honest with ya. These Americans sure like their brunch and Bloody Marys.

As a bartender you have to start out with the shitty shifts, so to speak, until you graduate to nights and then the good nights—weekday nights.

Well, I've finally graduated to those nights—the good nights—and now I'm off on Saturdays and Sundays. My new shifts behind the bar are Monday–Friday nights, six o'clock to whenever!

It turned out they were actually looking for a full-time bartender and were just training me until my confidence as a bartender improved.

Well, I'm hanging out at the bar one Sunday having a few Bloody Marys. I notice Billy, the weekend bartender, put vodka in my Bloody Mary. I say to this amateur, "Why are you putting vodka in my Bloody Mary?"

"You're supposed to put vodka in a Bloody Mary. You mean to tell me, you haven't been putting any booze in the Bloody Marys for the last few months?" he says.

"That's right," I say, to which the whole bar erupts with laughter and the boss gives me a wink and a nice whack on the back. Great profits when I work, ah.

What really amazed me about the whole thing was that nobody ever complained or ever sent one back. What's even funnier—all these fuckers who were laughing at me, making fun of me, are the same people whom I have been serving for the last few months and gypping them out of real Bloody Marys. Charging them six dollars for tomato juice. Who's the fuckin' eejit now?

By the way, Billy, the weekend day bartender, is quite the character. He's known as Doctor Bill, or the one I like the most—Billy Buy-Back. He's pretty generous with the free drinks. I guess he must be doing something right as he's been working behind this bar for over thirty years—since nineteen seventy, when the bar first opened. Also works up the street in one of the best dive bars in the city—the Holland Bar.

Anyway, I'm sitting having Sunday brunch, paying eighteen dollars for eggs, surrounded by a bunch of girls talking about flowers, curtains, and shopping. How about after brunch we go to a candle shop? Oh, can we, please. I'm so happy! Do you ever just want to flip the whole fuckin' table over? Do ya, Smithy? Ya, I'd rather get up early on my day off to listen to a bunch of women talk about the color of their curtains than sleep in and watch football. Sorry about the rant again, Smithy.

Remember how I told you there was a jewelry shop next to the bar? Well, it's not quite. I go in there the other day to buy something for my mother for Christmas. I tell the man behind the counter what I'm looking for, and he looks at me like I'm speaking another language. Now, I know I have an accent, but I'm still speaking English, or at least pretty close to it.

It looks like a jewelry shop. It even has jewelry in the shop window and pieces of jewelry hanging in the store. I tell the locals in the bar that night what happened, and they all start laughing again. There seems to be a trend developing here. Learned something new today. It's actually a betting shop, like a bookies in Ireland. Only thing about it is, betting shops are illegal in New York City. So they put up dummy jewelry to conceal the fact. For instance, the New York State Lottery gives you eight to one if you bet, whereas next door will give you ten to one or something like that. You bet the daily numbers, which is usually three or four numbers at a time. If your numbers are picked by the lottery, you win, and next door will give you the extra percentages. It makes total sense now as in the daytime there is always a queue outside, particularly from the employees from the post office a few streets away. I tried it, but no luck.

Smithy, you should come out for a holiday. We'll do brunch and have some Bloody Marys. I'll get Billy to make them.

THREE

Thursday, November 4, 1999
Hell's Kitchen

Getting really busy behind the bar these days, Smithy, as the summer is coming to a close. Making money, too—I've never had a comma in my bank account before. The summers in New York City are long and hot. I love them. I suppose coming from Ireland where it rains twice a week (once for three days and once for four days), it's hard not to love the weather over here.

You asked why they call the area where I work Hell's Kitchen. Well, I did some research and asked a few locals, and this is what they told me.

First, the area is roughly between Seventh Avenue and the Hudson River from Thirty-Fourth Street to Fifty-Seventh Street. I say "roughly" because depending on whom you talk to, it might be a block, a street, or an avenue here or there.

Hell's Kitchen was mostly an Irish and German community and was notorious for assaulting unwelcome intruders by raining down a storm of bricks, rocks, and paving stones from tenement rooftops with legendary accuracy.

Most discussions around the origin of the name center on whether "Hell's Kitchen" was first applied to a tenement, a rookery, a street, an incident, or a gang.

The boundaries of the original Hell's Kitchen were only between Thirty-Sixth and Forty-First Streets and Ninth Avenue and the Hudson River. Then eventually a larger area adopted the name.

Within this area were the most infamous tenements and rookeries (single-family homes, often dilapidated wooden shanties, converted to multi-family dwellings). It was an area of destitution infused with whiskey and prostitution, and, near the northeast corner of Thirty-Ninth Street and Tenth Avenue, was this multi-family shanty tenement dubbed "Hell's Kitchen."

Other theories I have been told by the locals include the idea that the term

Hell's Kitchen is a corruption of *Heil's Kitchen*, for a German lady who ran a restaurant near the docks. Another idea was that a news reporter coined the term in a story he was writing about the neighborhood. And the most-often repeated theory I hear says that it originated the night that Dutch Fred, a veteran police officer, was on patrol with a rookie cop on West Thirty-Ninth Street near Tenth Avenue (suspiciously close to the rookery of the same name). The two cops were witnessing a small riot and purportedly the rookie said to Dutch Fred, "This place is hell itself," to which the veteran cop replied, "Hell's a mild climate. This is Hell's Kitchen, no less."

Notable people who have grown up or lived in Hell's Kitchen include Larry David, James Dean, Bob Hope, Alicia Keys, Madonna, Frank Miller, Burt Reynolds, Jerry Seinfeld, Sylvester Stallone, and now me.

Well, there you have it, Smithy. Now you know. That's enough history for today. Talk soon, my friend, and get your arse out here to Hell's Kitchen.

FOUR

Tuesday, November 23, 1999
Where Did It All Begin?

I met this hot Asian girl named Nina at the bar. Fuck me, she's gorgeous. Attractive, thin, exotic-looking with soft black hair and olive skin. She seemed very pleasant, and I was immediately interested.

We don't see too many of them in Ireland, do we, Smithy? Real mysterious. Mind you, Canadians would seem exotic to the Irish. By the way, I think I'm going to take a trip up to Canada. I saw an advertisement today on the side of a bus that read "Drink Canada Dry," so I think I'll give it a shot.

Anyway, I'm not quite sure what it is, maybe you know, Smithy, but every Caucasian man wants to bang an Asian chick, and I'm not just some regular Caucasian man . . . I'm an Irish Caucasian. This is the stuff of fantasies. It's not just shaggin' a regular white chick. It's much more than banging a black chick. It's an Asian chick . . . a fuckin' Asian chick. It's like banging an alien.

She asks me where I am from. Well, Smithy, here's what I told her (ya know you have to fuck with people a wee bit when ya can; these Yanks would swallow a brick). One fella at the bar still thinks my uncle is a leprechaun. As a bartender, having a good story and a joke (the Irish are usually never short of either, as you know) is important and helps with the tips—you got to give them what they want.

Here's what I tell her: My childhood was pretty normal. My two fathers were very supportive! I actually grew up in an orphanage; I didn't want to, but my parents insisted. No, really, I grew up in a small house on the south side of Dublin, Ireland. Well, it was small because there were eight people in it. I'm the youngest of five boys and a girl. Although we have all very different personalities, we all share a passion for telling stories and having a laugh.

I think when you grow up in Dublin particularly, you grow up surrounded by great storytellers. I'm not talking about the obvious ones like Yeats, Joyce, and Behan, but your next-door neighbor and the old man at the end of the bar. I suppose we have all been affected and influenced by them, in one way or another.

My dad is actually a stand-up comic and was and still is very successful. However, when he was doing his thing on the stage, my mom was the real comedian in the house. My dad gave me my spirit, but my ma gave me my soul. Collectively they gave me my nose. I'm not saying it's large, but I can smoke under the shower.

The best piece of advice I ever got was from my mother. She told me one time, "Never go out with a girl with big hands." I say, "Why not, Mother?" "Because," she says, "it will make your dick look ri-dic-ulous"—pun most definitely intended.

When I was a kid I used to sleep in the same bed with two of my brothers—and both of them used to wet the bed. I learned how to swim by the time I was three. My mother used to say to me, "What part of the bed would you like to sleep in?" I would always say, "The shallow end, please." When I would wake up, there would be a rainbow at the end of the bed.

She used to tell me that every day was my birthday. However, I found out after, it was only to hide her addiction to cakes and balloons. She always wanted to get rid of me. She used to wrap my school lunch every day in a road map. Maybe that's why I love to travel.

We were kinda poor when we were growing up, as you can probably see and imagine. My mother would send me down to the local butcher shop and tell me to ask the butcher for a sheep's head. (They were cheap.) She would ask me to tell the butcher to leave one of the legs on, to cut it as close to its arse as possible, or tell him to leave the eyes in, as it has to see us through the week.

I was twelve when I got my first job. The only thing I remember is how many times my grandmother died. On one of my first jobs I was walking across the factory floor and the sole of my shoe was falling off. As I walked, everyone could hear it flapping on the ground. The boss walked by and said, "How come your sole is falling off?" I told him that I was waiting on my first week's wages so I could get it fixed. He said, "I'm so sorry," and he reached into his jacket and took out a big wad of cash, took the rubber band off, and said, "Here, that should get you by until Friday."

I would get hand-me-down clothes from all my older brothers and my sister—all the clothes they had grown out of. I remember getting hand-me-down trousers from my oldest brother one time. He was six foot two and I was five foot one. I had to open my fly to blow my nose. I remember wearing the same dress as my teacher. Mind you, I think he was more embarrassed than I was. My parents didn't have enough money to buy me a new suit for my confirmation, so my father bought me a new cap and told me to look out the window. But you know what—we were happy!

Thursday, December 2, 1999
Is New York City Really Safe?

Local police in Times Square arrested two skinheads last night. One swallowed battery acid and the other one ate fireworks. The police charged one and let the other one off.

The police station in Midtown South on Thirty-Fifth Street was broken into. All the toilet seats were stolen. When asked about the break-in, the police captain said, "We have nothing to go on."

A Polish man was stabbed forty-two times in the back tonight outside a city café. The police said it was the worst case of suicide they had ever seen.

So, are we really safe? I will let you make up your own mind. Personally this makes me feel about as safe as a gerbil in a Chelsea pet shop window!

I recently asked a mate of mine what he liked about New York City. He said, "What I like about NYC is that you can get beer and Buffalo wings at five in the morning." I think that sums it up. I'm sitting at home right now eating hot wings, writing this letter to you, Smithy. It's six o'clock in the morning. I got four cans of beer on my way home tonight. I'm almost finished, and I'm going down to the corner to get more. Then I'm going to go up to the roof and watch the city wake up.

It's the convenience of it all that we fall in love with.

Well, be safe, relax, have a beer, and always remember to tip your bartender.

Monday, December 13, 1999
Wankers

It's about ten o'clock, Smithy. The first rush of the night is over, awaiting the next one. It's slowly starting to fill up at the bar again. That's how it usually works. You get the after-work group waiting on their train or bus home. Then after they leave, you slowly start getting the night crowd—a mixture of tourists and locals.

This girlfriend of mine surprises me with a visit to the bar. We are chatting between customers when I notice this Mexican guy come in and sit in the corner of the bar across from her. I know he's Mexican because half of Mexico is working in our kitchen. I welcome him in as he asks for a Corona. Actually I was reading in the *New York Daily News* today that Mexicans are the happiest people in the world—I think that's because most of them live in America. There are a lot of Mexicans in New York and America. I can't say I blame them, considering they live below a place called New Mexico. If I was still living in Ireland and there was a place called New Ireland or Better Ireland, I would go, as well. I'm sure if Canada was called New America, it would be full of Americans—until the winter rolled in, anyway. Mexicans come to America because the grass is greener, and Americans go to Mexico because the grass is legal and better.

The bar starts to fill up a bit more, and I start to get busy. About twenty minutes pass, and I finally get everybody served. I go back to the end of the bar to see how Emily is doing. As I walk down the bar I notice a horrified look on her face, as she is glaring uncomfortably at the Mexican guy sitting across from her. I look at him only to see him playing with himself, his dick in his hand. I grab his "drink"—don't get ahead of me—and tell him to get the fuck out of the bar. "You sick little fucker." He comes all over the place. I've never seen so much—maybe he just got out of prison? He runs out the door while pulling his trousers up. That wasn't the tip I was hoping for.

I was reading in the paper that a man actually got arrested for masturbating. I mean, has the world gone crazy, getting arrested for masturbating. If that was the case, I should be on death row!

That reminds me, it's actually a little bit embarrassing. When I was a kid, my dad walked into my bedroom unexpectedly only to catch me playing with myself. He says to me, "Son, if you don't stop playing with yourself you will go blind." I was like, "Dad, I'm sitting over here."

I actually walked in on my brother one time when he was wanking—on my bleedin' bed, too. He's like, "Are you mad?" "No," I say, "but you seem to be." There's a time and a place for everything. Please do your wanking (masturbating) at home and not on my bed or in my bar.

Dad, Tom, the cop—Dublin 1960
On the first day he spent on the beat
in Dublin, he found a dead horse in
Exchequer Street, couldn't spell it, and
had to drag it around into Dame Street.

Dad, Tom (Shaun Connors), the comedian

The Lads: my brothers, Steve, Tommy, Joe, and John

With my siblings: Karen (she still wears that jumper), John, Steve, Joe, and Tom

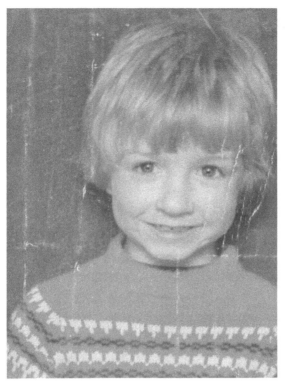

Wee Barry

My first football team—Broadford Rovers. I'm bottom row,
first on the left, my dad is standing far right, and pro golfer
Padraig Harrington, the goalie, top row, third from the left.

My mother, Dolores (second from the right),
out with friends, Dublin 1958

At my brother Tommy's wedding. You have to get married sometime—
you can't spend your whole life being happy. Left to right: me, John,
Joe, Steve, Dad, Tommy, and my favorite sister, Karen.
(Only half of us got the memo to smile.)

FIVE

Sunday, April 16, 2000
Midtown South Police Station

Today I bought a car from a lad from the neighborhood for eight hundred dollars. The local cops from Midtown South promised me a parking pass to put in the window. It's a NYPD pass that you put in your window letting you pretty much park anywhere. So that means I can park on the street for free. Trust me, Smithy, that's a great deal, as parking in this city is a nightmare and expensive. It can be as much as four hundred dollars a month to park in a garage. Pretty sweet deal, hey, Smithy. I have it parked on Thirty-Sixth Street across from my flat. Probably will never use it, mind ya. You really don't need a car in the city, as the public transportation is so good, but with a deal like that I couldn't pass it up.

Because the bar is so close to the Midtown South Police Station on Thirty-Fifth Street we get a lot of cops coming in. A wild bunch, but real heroes in this city as far as I'm concerned. In my short time here, the local police have certainly helped me out on more than one occasion.

Late night at the bar they like to shoot off their guns in the ceiling. It can get pretty crazy at times. I'm standing by the bathroom the other night, putting some songs on the jukebox, when right beside me a cop whips out his gun and puts a couple of bullets in the ceiling. For the rest of the night I couldn't hear a fuckin' thing.

There is an office above the bar, but it's empty at night so it's "somewhat" safe. The bar is well known for this. When "newbies" come in, they usually want to add to the history and so like to put their own bullet hole in the well-shot-up tin ceiling. "Let me have a go," I said to one of the rookies, and I put my own piece of history in the ceiling. I wonder, will that be my last?

It's the oldest bar in the neighborhood with many stories and even more bullet holes.

I love it when the older cops or retired cops come in. The first thing they do as they walk into the bar is look up to the ceiling, replaying past stories and memories, I'm sure.

Things are not as wild as they once were, for obvious reasons.

One cop was telling me this funny story a few weeks ago.

A bunch of them came into the bar one Saturday morning after work. They had been doing the midnight to 8 a.m shift. About twelve o'clock in the afternoon they all decided to go outside and play football—American football, that is. Full of beer, they cordoned off Ninth Avenue between Thirty-Third and Thirty-Fourth Streets and started playing football. Now, we're not talking about a small backstreet in the middle of nowhere, or like when we used to play football on the streets outside our houses in Dublin, Smithy. This is a major, active street in Manhattan, New York City. After about an hour the police show up to see what's going on. They had been getting a lot of calls about the noise and traffic buildup. They show up to see the Midtown South Police Station having a game of football—what a surprise, I'm sure. They have a wee chat with their fellow cops and decide to open up *one* of the four lanes to let some traffic pass. Then they go back to their game. Nice compromise—fuckin' brilliant!

Tuesday, July 25, 2000
Hot in the City Tonight

It's hot today in the city, Smithy—like a hair dryer on high hitting you right in the kisser. I'm sweating like R. Kelly at a Girl Scout meeting, like an Israeli bus driver, like a priest at a Boy Scout meeting, like Britney Spears on *Jeopardy.* You got it right—I was sweating.

They say it's all that global warming stuff—who knows? I heard the actor Vin Diesel, in support of global warming, has changed his name from Vin Diesel to Vin Ethanol. Well done, Vin, it all helps.

At least the homeless people in New York City are pleased with the longer warmer months. I actually only date homeless people because when the date is over you can drop them off anywhere.

Where our bar is, Smithy, you get a lot of homeless people because we are behind Penn Station—the train station on Thirty-Third Street, and near Port Authority—the bus station on Forty-Second Street.

I feel bad for the homeless; they are harmless for the most part, and I try to help them out the best I can. You know what, most of them just want people to recognize them, to acknowledge them. To look them in the eye and say hello. Honestly. I find when I do that they appreciate it, their faces light up a bit (even if it's just for a second or two), and they usually say thanks. They just want to feel normal, I think. They can be quite funny. This homeless lad walked into the bar last night, wheeling his carry-on baggage like he was going on a plane and heading to an important meeting somewhere. He sits down at a table and says to me, "Can you put on the tennis?" I thought that was funny. If it wasn't for the fact that it was so busy or that he smelled of piss and crap I would have put it on for him and let him sit there for a while. That's not so good for business. "Sorry, mate, but you gotta go. Take care. Come back later."

It has given me a real proximity to humility, and it makes you realize how lucky you are.

That reminds me, Smithy; this man comes into the bar and sits by the window. It's basically just off Ninth Avenue. Well, I notice that every time a truck goes by the window, he starts shaking uncontrollably, and when you can't hear the truck anymore, he calms down and stops shaking. So I ask him, "Why every time a truck goes by do you start shaking uncontrollably?" He says, "Well, it's because my wife ran off with a truck driver, and every time I hear a truck go by, I think he's bringing her back . . . ."

You could not make this shite up, Smithy, even if you wanted to.

a transvestite, and now we are in an S&M club. Is there a pattern starting to develop?

Well, as I told you, Smithy, we were both pissed so we decided to check it out further. First thing—where's the bar?

Jeff asks for a Guinness. (Ah, God bless his enthusiasm!) The nice fella behind the bar who's only wearing one sock—and it's not on his foot—says, "We only sell cocktails." (All pun intended yet again.) Jeff decides on a purple motherfucker (blue curacao, Southern Comfort, amaretto, and cranberry juice), and I get a green one (rum and green crème de menthe and something else, I think). He states that in here you can enjoy any fantasy of your choice at reasonable prices. Foot fetish parties in the private room in the back, paddle spanking catered to every desire, and human carpet parties and bondage in the private dungeon. I'm sure they have a reach-around party behind the dumpster in the back.

We're standing at the bar drinking these ridiculous cocktails, looking like a bunch of gobshites, with naked people everywhere. The dance floor is jam-packed with everyone doing the "behind grind," and some are doing it for real. It was like a Village People reunion. Like a piñata exploded. I head off to the jacks, and as I open the door I see that the floor is see-through and people are swimming underneath me. Nice touch—very classy. I walk up to the urinal to find a naked masked man chained to it. I would be, too—masked, that is. I wouldn't want anyone to recognize me, either. He asks me if I would be so kind and piss on him. When in Rome—so I gave him a wee tinkle. I got stage fright, I suppose. That's all I could manage—a tinkle. Funny, I was bursting for a piss earlier. By the way, the lads who were swimming underneath were swimming in piss. All the urine was collecting underneath. I leave and head back to the bar to see Jeff. He says, "You'll never guess what somebody just asked me." "Jeff, anything you say to me right now wouldn't surprise me." "Well, somebody just asked me if I would pee in their drink." "Jeff, go into the bathroom and I will pay the check," I say.

What a bleedin' laugh, Smithy. Talk about taking the piss!

Thursday, June 21, 2001
Funny Bar Story

This Irishman walked into the bar a few weeks ago and ordered three pints of Guinness. He picks up all three pints and sits in the back of the bar, drinking a sip out of each one in turn. When he's finished all three, he comes back to the bar and orders three more. I said to him, "You know, a pint goes flat after I pull it. It would taste better if you bought one at a time." He replies, "Well, ya see, I have two brothers. One is in Australia, the other's in Dublin, and I'm here in New York City. When we all left home, we promised that we'd drink this way to remember the days when we all drank together when we were all back in Dublin." I said, "That's a wonderful custom," and I left it there. He has become a regular over the last few months and always drinks the same way: orders three pints of Guinness and drinks the three pints by taking sips from each of them in turn.

Well, last night he came in and ordered two pints. All the regulars and myself notice and we all fall silent. Our hearts dropped. When he comes back to the bar for a second round, I say to him, "I don't want to intrude on your grief, but I want to offer my condolences to you on your great loss." He looks at me, confused for a moment, then a light dawns in his eyes and he laughs. "Oh, no," he says to me. "Everyone is fine. It's me . . . I've quit drinking."

You meet them all at the bar, Smithy, that's for sure.

By the way, these two Irish lads walk out of a bar—it could happen!

SEVEN

Tuesday, September 11, 2001

Well, Smithy, we all know what happened on this day, the worst and, more importantly, the best of humanity. It has all been well-documented; no need for me to get into it. However, on a personal note, what I remember most is the best of humanity that day and the days, weeks, months, and years to follow. As the Towers fell, Smithy, so many rose. Immediately after September eleventh, the whole city stopped and was eerily silent. The taxi cabs stopped blowing their horns constantly, people opened doors for each other, and people in general were a little bit more patient and courteous toward each other. Then within minutes—it seemed so, anyway—people from around the country and around the world just started showing up on our doorstep to help in whatever way they could. Because my bar is so close to the Midtown South Police Precinct, all the volunteers would be brought in by the local police for some food and a beer in between volunteering at Ground Zero. We were open pretty much twenty-four hours a day for months after the events of September eleventh. The people I met over that time will stay with me forever. That's why I say that it was the worst and best of humanity. The volunteers wanted nothing but to get back down there and help, usually with little or no sleep. The firemen and women, the police, and all the many volunteers who came to help—they were true heroes, and I will never forget them. I miss ya, Kim.

Monday, October 22, 2001
Where's the Whiskey?

My good friend comes in tonight. He's a cop in Midtown South. Let's call him Dutch, after the legendary NYC cop—Dutch Fred.

I see he has mischief in his eyes and thirst in his belly. The last time I saw this look, he left his gun in my apartment. It was actually rather funny. A couple of weeks ago I decided to have a wee party. Maybe ten people. About six or seven people are chatting in the living room, and another few people are in the kitchen. I look over at the coffee table and count two guns and a set of handcuffs—can't help but chuckle to myself. I'm pouring shots of tequila for everyone. A couple of hours pass and I decide to call it a night. I leave the rest of them in the living room, and my date and I go to bed. I get up to take a piss, and as I'm walking past the coffee table I notice that there are still two guns and a set of handcuffs on it. Everybody is gone. Then, sure enough, my phone starts ringing, and eventually the front door is buzzing. "Hey, I think we left our guns with you." "Ya, come on up, I'll leave the door unlocked." I went back to bed. No harm, no foul, right?

Anyway, Monday nights are always good to go out because a lot of people who work in the bar and restaurant business seem to be out on these nights. You meet a lot of people you know and people whom you have a lot in common with. It's good craic. It's midnight and the crowd is thinning out—perfect. There's me and Dutch and three women left at the bar. I buy everyone a shot of whiskey, and I suggest that we all go downtown. The girls are up for it, so I finish up the cash, do a quick clean, then grab a few beers and a bottle of whiskey for the ride down. We all pile into Dutch's unmarked police car. The three girls in the back are snickering with excitement. We make a right onto Thirty-Third Street and a left onto the West Side Highway, passing the bottle around as we head south. Dutch says, "Hold my gun, will you? It's pinching me," as he throws it on my lap. Not the first time I've seen or held his gun. The whiskey comes back around for the third time, and now I'm feeling no pain. I have a brilliant idea, and I hold his gun out the window and fire three shots in the air, thinking I'm a cowboy or something. Dutch is laughing as we continue down the highway. Sure enough, about a minute later we see flashing lights behind us. Thinking that it's an ambulance, we slow down and move over to the side, only to see the lights follow us. It's the highway police, and now there are about five more cars quickly moving in. Dutch pulls over to the side and puts his hands on top of the steering wheel. "Hide everything," he says. I'm wiping his gun with my shirt as I slip it under the seat, trying to get any evidence of me off it. Next minute there are cops everywhere surrounding the car with their guns drawn. I was bricking it—can't imagine how the girls were feeling. "Out of the car!" they scream. "Get out of the car!" Dutch gets out explaining, "I'm a cop, I'm a cop." Then one of the cops says, "Dutch, what the fuck." "I'm sorry, guys, just letting off some steam, sorry." Finally the tension eases, they put their guns down and turn around, shaking their heads as they walk away. Dutch gets back in and we screech off. "I'm sorry, Dutch," I say. "Don't worry about it. Where's the whiskey?" he says.

Eventually we make it down to the Seaport area in Lower Manhattan, after the inconvenience of being pulled over by the highway police. The great thing about driving in an unmarked police car is that we can pretty much park anywhere. We park the car outside Jeremy's Ale House on Front Street—right in front of a fire hydrant. It's a wild country-and-western-style bar. Great craic. After no time, we are all immersed in the atmosphere of the bar and the people in it. Most of the people know Dutch already, so the beers and shots are flowing yet again. The girls are digging it and are up on top of the bar dancing away. Fair play to them! Shot—okay. Beer—okay. Shot—okay. Shots and beers are flowing. The craic is ninety.

I eyeball a pool table in the corner and head over to see if there's any action. I throw a few games, but I'm eventually up about sixty bucks. All those days spent in the pool hall, skipping school, are finally paying off. I beat this lad badly who was showing off earlier (which was a mistake), and now he's not very happy. I have just taken forty dollars off him. He's with a bunch of his friends, and now I have just humiliated him in front of them. First rule in pool: know who you're up against. The tension is starting to build as they start whispering to each other. I'm just playing the game and trying to convince this fucker that I just got lucky when Dutch comes over and puts his gun on the table and says, "Everyone okay here?" Dutch is either totally insane or totally committed to life. Maybe it's the same thing or a combination of both.

The sun is now peeping through the only piece of the window that is not covered. This is when I realize it's probably time to call it a night. "Thanks, lads," I say as I pick up my money and walk over to the bar. Lo and behold, the girls are long gone. I was too busy playing pool in the corner. A curse of my youth.

Well, we leave the car outside and take a taxi back to Hell's Kitchen.

By the way, I think Dutch is committed to life. I learned something that night! He's a good man.

EIGHT

Friday, November 16, 2001
Scottish Stevie

Friday nights are always fun and busy. It's about ten o'clock when in walk these four Scottish lads. I know they're Scottish because I can hear them squeak. The Scots are known to be cheap. They squeak when they walk. As tight as a nun's arse. They invented copper wire; it was two Scotsmen fighting over a penny. I love the Scots except when they want to fight. They are worse than the Irish when it comes to fighting—remember, they invented the Glasgow Kiss. That's another story.

I meet John, Pat, Craig, and Stevie. Three Celtic soccer fans and one Rangers fan. As you know, Smithy, Celtic being Catholics and Rangers being Protestants. It's unusual to see them hanging out together. It's a big rivalry in Scotland, never mind the whole religious aspect of the whole thing. In America it's like the Lakers and Celtics in basketball or the Yankees and the Red Sox in baseball—only a hundred times worse.

Personally I don't give a shite about it all, and I'm happy to see Celtic and Rangers fans partying together. Stevie tells me a joke that pretty much sums up what I'm talking about—here it goes, and there is nothing quite like a Scotsman and his big, powerful, barely understandable accent, telling a joke or story. We're cut from the same cloth, after all.

Celtic and Rangers are playing each other in the Rangers' (Protestant) home park. During the chaos that happens entering an intense local rivalry like this, a Celtic fan happens to get caught in the Rangers' crowd and the Rangers fans' part of the stadium. He zips up his jacket so that the Rangers fans can't see his Celtic green and white colors. The game is going well for Celtic, and sure enough they score. With that the Celtic fan jumps up to celebrate the goal, only to realize that he is in the wrong end. So this big Rangers fan standing next to him says, "Go get me a beer and leave one of your boots here so that I know you will come back." While the Celtic fan is getting him a beer, the Rangers fan shites in his boot. Well, the Celtic fan comes back, gives the Rangers fan his beer, and steps back into his boot. He is disgusted by what he finds, but he knows he has to stay. Sure enough, Celtic scores again and he jumps up to celebrate again, only to realize again he is in the wrong end. Again he goes for the beer, and again the Rangers fan shites into his other boot. The game ends 2-0 for Celtic, and the Celtic fan makes it out alive. As he is walking down the street leaving the stadium, a camera crew from CNN comes up to him and asks him if the rivalry between Celtic and Rangers will ever end. "No," the Celtic supporter says. "I don't think the rivalry will ever change. As long as they keep shitting in our boots and we keep pissing in their beers."

You can use that joke for any of the sports rivalries around the world. Try it—give it a shot!

Well, anyway, we all hit it off and arrange to meet the next day and have a drunken weekend together. Stevie and I in particular hit it off, and from then on Stevie would just show up from time to time at the bar on a Friday night, knowing that I would be off for the next two days—Saturday and Sunday. Whenever I would see Stevie walk through the door of the bar, I would say to myself, *Oh fuck, here we go again.* But deep down I'm always excited to see him and for the shenanigans to begin.

I get a call one night from John Collins, Stevie's mate. He tells me Stevie is dying of cirrhosis of the liver and he maybe has six months to live. Stevie shows up at the bar two weeks later with the usual thirst in his eyes and belly. After a few pints I tell Stevie about the call and tell him I can't be involved with him killing himself.

I say to Stevie, "Fuck this, you're a young man (he was 38), and you have your whole life ahead of you." I leave him at the bar. He calls me the next day. We meet at the Cheyenne Diner on Ninth and Thirty-Third Street and have our usual breakfast at noon. We have a real heart-to-heart, and he basically explains to me that he's had a great life, he's happy, both his parents are dead, his sister's taken care of, and he just wants to have fun. Again, I say, "Fuck that, Stevie, you have so much to live for." Again he says, "I've lived the life of twenty people. Let me do what I want to do."

Well, who am I to decide his fate when he obviously has already made up his mind? I say, "Okay, let's go, Stevie, and have some fun. Let's get pissed; let's go and fuckin' kill ya." We head across town to Paddy Reilly's bar, one of Stevie's favorite bars, on Twenty-Ninth and Second Avenue. We get there at around 2 p.m. and we order the usual: two pints of Guinness and two shots of whiskey. Amy is already working on the Guinness as we walk up to the bar. What we like about this bar is that it's a quiet daytime drinking place where you can hide away from the world and have great pints and whiskey at reasonable prices. Not to mention the live music they have every day. We are there about two hours. As normal, Stevie and I have gotten to know everybody at the bar. We are probably on our third round of whiskeys and Guinness when I notice this rather large man walk into the bar. He squeezes in next to me and orders, what else, a pint of Guinness and a shot of whiskey. I say, "Ah man, good on ya, that's what we are drinking." It's at this point I look at Stevie and whisper, "You know who the fuck that is sitting beside me?" "Who is it, you crazy fucker?" he says. "That's Norm from *Cheers*, you know, what's-his-face, oh, that's right, George Wendt, the fat fucker, no offense, Stevie, from the show *Cheers*." Well, with that, Stevie is fuckin' loving it. Stevie, being Stevie, leans over and says, "From one fat fucker to another, great to see you have good taste, *Cheers*." We all *clink* our pints. "Can I buy you a drink?" Stevie says. I say to Stevie, "That's six words you will never hear in Scotland: Can I buy you a drink?" "Ya smart cunt," he says (remember, *cunt* is a nice word on the right side of the Atlantic), "and fuck you" (or as he pronounces it, "Fuk ye"). Stevie uses the words "brand new" all the time, pronounced "*bran nu*"—meaning, you're all right. Well, Norm turns into a riot and great craic. He accepts Stevie's offer, and from then on we were inseparable for the rest of the day and night, going round for round until four o'clock in the morning. I have to say, I will never forget it. From start to finish, as normal, we laugh our fuckin' arses off, talking about Stevie growing up in Glasgow, me in Dublin, and our new friend Norm telling us all his showbiz stories. It's one of the best and funniest nights of my life—thanks, Stevie. A week later I get a call from John telling me Stevie had died.

I go over to Glasgow for the funeral and, not surprisingly, the church is packed. A lot of drunk Scots in kilts playing bagpipes. There's nothing quite as haunting as hearing the bagpipes, particularly at a funeral. By the way, what's the difference between an onion and the bagpipes? Nobody cries when you chop up a bagpipe. Stevie will be mad at me for that one. RIP, mate.

I stopped by his friend John's house and I noticed that he was taking the wallpaper off the walls. I say to him, "Are you decorating?" "No," he says, "I'm moving." We went down to see the famous museum and statue of William Wallace in Stirling. (Remember *Braveheart*, freedom and all that?) So we were in Stirling and this man comes up to me and says, "Do you know where the statue of Mel Gibson is?" I won't say who said it, but to be fair to this American guy, the statue does look a bit like him.

Stevie Byrne, George Wendt (Norm from *Cheers*), and Me

NINE

Tuesday, March 12, 2002
Green Card

Well, back in New York City again, after my trip to Scotland—I'm bloody broke. You'll find that happens when you spend time in Scotland—a place that has the most crowded taxi cabs in the world! I'm glad to be back in New York City. Sometimes you have to leave New York to realize how amazing it is, and how much I miss and love this city. It's the only place where I can be truly alone, if I want to be.

I walk into my apartment, and Randy, my roommate, is sitting at the kitchen table with a big fuckin' smug look on his face. Whenever I see this look on his face, I know I'm in trouble. He has this big, brown, official-looking envelope in his hand. He throws it at me saying, "Yankee, this is for you." It has an INS symbol on it—Immigration and Naturalization Services. "Holy shite, is this what I think it is?" Ya, it's my green card application saying that I have been approved. I have to go to the American Embassy in Dublin. Fuck, I just came from there. But I'm obviously over the moon. Fuckin' brilliant. Randy has a bottle of Jack Daniels opened up, and we are now toasting my imminent citizenship—I hope, anyway. He says, "Now that you are going to be an American, you need to start drinking American whiskey." I hate the stuff, but what ya gonna do?

I need to be back in Dublin by the end of the month, the letter says. Remember, Smithy: I'm broke after my last trip and not working behind the bar for a few weeks. Randy says, "Listen, I will give you the money, no problem. I know you're broke." "Thanks a lot, Randy," I say. I know Randy can be a real bollox, or "ball buster," as they say in America (after all, I'm almost an American now), but he has always been there for me. Again he says, "No problem, I will give you the money. Just run downstairs and grab me a pack of cigarettes." We have a convenient store right underneath our apartment—very convenient. So I grab the money on the table, and just before I leave the apartment he says, "Slow down, hold on a second. You need to go down naked and grab me some cigarettes—you never let me finish." "What, fuck off, would ya? No way! I'm not going down there onto Ninth Avenue in the buff. Especially in this weather!" It's March in NYC—its fuckin' bitter cold. It's a couple of degrees short of freezing to death. "I'm not doing it, and by the way, Randy, you're a cunt." Then I just sit back down at the coffee table. Randy repeats it again: "Listen, all you have to do is run downstairs naked and get me a pack of smokes. That's it. And if you do that, I will pay for your trip. It would be no fun if I just gave you the money without you doing something for it, now would it? It will be a good story, at least."

"I'll get bleedin' arrested if I run out there naked." "Don't worry," Randy says. "Nobody will see it anyway. If you're arrested they'll probably take you to *small* claims court." Cheeky bollox.

Now, the Jack is starting to flow. I'm loosening up, but I'm still not going to leave this apartment naked. I'm not that loose. Well, before you know it, I'm drunk and thinking to myself, *I just need to run down three flights of stairs, run into the store right next to our door, and get smokes—naked.* Now I'm seriously thinking about it. What do I have to lose? He will buy me a return ticket to Ireland to get my green card. I jump up, take a big swig of Jack, take my clothes off, grab the money for the cigs, and run out the door. I chicken out once I get to the staircase. Run back in to see Randy laughing, rolling around on the couch. "You're a prick," I say as he continues to laugh. "Fuck it." I run out again and make it to the front door of the apartment building only to chicken out again when I see all the people walking by on Ninth Avenue. I run back upstairs only to find the apartment door is now locked. Randy locked the door! The prick has locked me out. I'm now naked in the hallway, locked out of my own apartment. Well, fuck it, I take a deep breath, run down again for the third time now, run out the door, make a very quick right, turn into the very convenient store—particularly today. I ask Mohamed for pack of Marlboros. "Keep the change!" I shout as I throw him ten dollars, grab the smokes, and run out the door followed by a series of laughs as I exit. I did it. "Fuck ya, Randy—I did it."

A lot of people do many things in order to become citizens of America. Mexicans risk their lives coming across the border. I'm sure if you looked at the Mexican-American border at night with night goggles on, it would look like the start of the NYC marathon. All I had to do was to run naked into a store on Ninth Avenue and get some smokes! Happy days.

TEN

Nina comes in tonight, you know, the Asian chick I've wanted to shag for a while now.

She walks over to me, with her brother Doug in tow, kisses me, and gives me a hug so close that the sides of her breasts are rubbing my arms. I notice a sexy glint in her eye. She means business tonight. I think it's on!

They start on the shots right away. Not to be unsociable, as you know, I have a few car bombs with them—half pint of Guinness with a combined shot of Bailey's and whiskey dropped right in. Her brother heads off—thank God (fucking cock blocker). Now it's pretty much just Nina and me, except for a few stragglers at the end of the bar.

Next thing Nina says, "You wanta hang out tonight?" "Okay, last call, everyone. Time to go home."

Before we know it, it's just the two of us—4:30 in the morning, time to go. I suggest to her that we head down to Chinatown, where I know she lives, and get some food. I mention one of my favorite twenty-four-hour joints called Wo Hops on Mott Street. She knows the place well—great. We walk outside and it's lashing rain. Nina shelters under the canopy of the bar, and I'm out on the street trying to hail down a cab. There are plenty of cabs going by but none stopping. Made me feel like a black man. I'm fucking soaking wet, flailing my arms around like a windmill trying to get a taxi. No luck. Then I realize, sure, I have my car parked up the street—the one that I haven't moved since I bought it. I leave Nina outside the bar and I leg it up the street, jumping over the puddles. I pull up within minutes outside the bar and Nina jumps in. We drive down Ninth Avenue, which turns into Hudson Street, make a left on Canal Street and a right on Mott Street. Wo Hops is on the right. We make it to the restaurant in no time, get a parking spot right outside, and walk down the steps into the restaurant.

By the way, Smithy, what is it about Chinese restaurants? As soon as you walk in, they bleedin' attack you. "Waw ya want?" Screaming at the top of their lungs. "Waw ya want? You tell me waw ya want!" I'm like, "Can you give me time to chink?"

I know that was an inappropriate joke, particularly when I'm with Nina, but she laughed, so fuck off. If you think it's inappropriate, yup, then it's funny.

We're chowing down some Szechuan chicken and having a couple of green beers, when Nina leans over and whispers to me, "Take me home." CHECK PLEASE!

We walk about ten blocks and make it to her apartment down this already bustling Chinatown street. I forget the name. We get into her apartment and before we know it, we're in the scratcher. Right away she turns into a kinky little fucker. Nina starts throwing me around her bed like a little rag doll. As I said, "kinky little fucker." Then again, for the second time tonight, she whispers softly in my ear, "Do you want to tie me up? I really like it." As she is saying this, she reaches under her bed and grabs out some ropes and hand-cuffs. "I love America." It's not really my thing, but what the fuck. When in Chinatown, right?

I've never done well with knots, mind ya. I was kicked out of the Boy Scouts, remember, Smithy.

Anyway, some of it comes back to me and I finally get her legs tied up and her hands handcuffed. We're getting into it when for some reason I remember that my car needs to be moved by seven thirty. I see her alarm clock on the nightstand reads 7:23. I have seven minutes. You have what they call in New York City, Smithy, "alternate side parking," when on certain days you basically just need to move your car to the other side of the street so the street cleaners can do their thing. If you don't they will have your car towed away. A real pain in the arse, especially when you're in the middle of a shag. Remember, this is New York; if I tried to stop them from towing my car, they'd shoot me and leave me in the street as a warning to others. If you're lying dead in the parking space, you still have to put money in the meter, or they will tow your body.

As I begin to untie Nina's legs, she stops me and says, "Move your car and leave me tied up—it will be kinky. You can come back and save me." "What . . . are you sure?" I say. "Ya," she says. "Get your wee Irish arse back here real soon and rescue me!" Trying to imitate an Irish accent—very cute.

Wow, that's hot, I think to myself as I head out the door in search of my car. I find the car after a little search, as I remembered parking it outside the restaurant. Then I drive around for about ten minutes until I find another parking spot and then head back to Nina's apartment to "rescue her." As I'm walking back to her place, I start to get a sickening feeling in my gut. Like, I don't know where she lives or how to get back to her place—it all looks the same. Particularly in Chinatown. Fuck, I'm lost. Where the fuck am I?

I continue to walk around the streets, going up one street and down the next. Then up a different street, I think, getting more and more confused and lost. Then I think I recognize a street. But then I don't remember the building or apartment number. I'm waiting outside this building that I think Nina might be in, hoping that someone will come out. Waiting for an opportunity to quickly slip inside before any questions are asked. I start thinking to myself, *Exactly what am I going to offer in the way of an explanation, anyway?* "Hey, I left this girl tied up because I had to move my car. Will you let me back inside so I can finish killing her and robbing her place? And maybe if I have time, I can do you a wee bit later on. Thanks a lot."

Finally I do it the New York City way and slide my hand across the panel of numbers and start pressing all the buttons. Again, not even sure if it's the right building. I get a lot of "fuck offs," I assume, as most of them are in Chinese, until someone buzzes me into the building. I don't remember the floor or the apartment number. Again, not even sure it's the right building. I just wander around knocking on doors I think Nina is in. The one thing about NYC, Smithy, is somebody could be getting murdered outside your apartment and nobody would come out. Everybody keeps to themselves, especially in Chinatown. Then I realize, sure, she's fuckin' tied up; how is she going to answer the door anyway for fuck's sake? Knocking on doors and getting no answers, I continue wandering the halls for what seemed like hours until I finally decide to abandon my futile efforts for Nina and leave. We didn't plan this out very well. Fuck, I hope Nina is okay.

I wrote my beautiful Asian friend a poem in the hopes of when I see her again to say sorry—"Cing Cong, Cing Cong, Cing, Cing Cong, Cing Cing." I hope she likes it; I worked on it all night.

I told my mate this story and he says to me, "You're going to piss off more Asian people with this story than Hiroshima." Funny fucker, ah?

But seriously, Smithy, I haven't seen her since. Hope to fuck she has a roommate.

Friday, June 7, 2002
My Doctors' Appointment Today

Today was my annual doctor's appointment, Smithy. It's up on 125th Street in Harlem. What a very cool part of Manhattan. This is where the true color of NYC lives. I'm not saying that because a lot of black and Spanish people live up here. I mean the "colorful" people live here. For me it's where the "real" New Yorkers are. The "characters," as we say in Dublin. There's a great atmosphere—the place is alive with activity. Whether it's the street vendors that line the sidewalks of 125th Street, the legendary Apollo Theater, or the great food and atmosphere, particularly at Dinosaur BBQ, underneath the West Side Highway, Harlem is alive, and I love the beat up there. Anyway, back to my doctor's appointment.

It's always a little scary going for my yearly checkup. The life of a bartender is usually not that healthy. All those late nights, early mornings, beers, and shots. On your feet all the time, eating unhealthy fried food, and so on—you get the picture. I like to eat healthy, but it's difficult. When you're busy behind the bar, you don't get time to sit down and enjoy a healthy meal. It's usually grabbing something quick, which is often fried, as you're running around.

Mind you, nothing is as unhealthy and bad as my dad's cooking. When he cooked we usually ended up giving it to the dog under the table. I looked down one time to see the dog licking his arse. My dad says, "What's the dog doing?" I say, "I think he's trying to get the taste out of his mouth." Dad used smoke detectors as timers.

Anyway, back to my doctor's appointment again. I go into the doctor's office today like every year, feeling a wee bit scared and uneasy, hoping everything will be all right. I say to the doctor, "When I touch my head it hurts. When I touch my left arm and right knee it hurts, too. Pretty much wherever I touch, it hurts." He examines me and says, "You have a broken finger."

He says, "I'm going to need a blood sample, a urine sample, and a stool sample." I say, "Here . . . just take my underpants."

I think my doctor might be gay. "Why?" you ask, Smithy. He said to me, "Can you please take off all your clothes?" Then I said to him, "Where should I put them?" He says, "In the corner, on top of mine." Now come on, that's a little weird, right? That puts a whole new spin on the doctor saying, "This might hurt a little bit." Well, he continues to examine me. He says, "You need to stop masturbating." I ask, "Why?" and he says, "Because I'm trying to examine you."

He said I needed to exercise more. I told him, "I get enough exercise pushing my luck."

I passed with flying colors, and then I read in *The New York Times* today that flying colors cause cancer—I'm scared!

By the way, I had a Pop-Tart today, Smithy; my doctor told me I have to eat more fruit—feeling great.

Well, I survived another year. Here's to another year of the same old stuff, and remember, please . . . always tip your bartender.

ELEVEN

Tuesday, July 2, 2002
"Give Me Your Money, Motherfucker!"

What a night, Smithy. I guess you can tell by the headline "Give Me Your Money, Motherfucker!" that it wasn't a fun, ordinary night behind the bar. Not even close. Here's what happened.

It's about three forty-five in the morning and I'm trying to get fuckers out of the bar. It was a busy night. I finally get everybody out and start the process of cleaning up, counting money and coins, and getting the register and bar ready for the next day's business. I'm about to come out from behind the bar to lock the door as the last customers have just left. I'm a little slow in locking the door tonight—not sure why. I normally lock the door right after the last person steps out of the bar and onto the street on Ninth Avenue, but for whatever reason this night I get a wee bit lazy. Just as I'm about to come around the end of the bar, this guy comes in and asks me if I'm still open. I say, "No, we're closed."

Right away I have a bad feeling about this, and I know I'm in trouble. Again I say, "We're closed," a little more forceful. You know that sinking feeling you get in your gut just before something bad happens? This is when he pulls a gun out of his pocket, and my stomach just drops. My heart nearly stopped—actually, I'm pretty sure it did stop for three or four seconds. He points the gun right at me and screams, "Give me your money, motherfucker! Give me your money, motherfucker!"

I know, I'm now in serious trouble. Putting my hands up, I say, "No problem. I will give you whatever you need." (Even though inside I'm fuckin' brickin' it.) I go back to the register to take the money out when I notice two heads in the back of the restaurant. I remember all of a sudden that there are two detectives back there. They came in earlier, and I totally forgot about them. I can see them but he can't, as they are in a booth in the very back section of the restaurant. They don't move or say anything; they are just observing what's going on. (Remember what I told you before, Smithy: the bar is close to the Midtown South Police Station, so we get a lot of cops and detectives in.)

I take the sleeve out of the register and leave it on the bar. I can see this prick is sweating like fuck and is obviously on something, which makes it even worse and unpredictable. I leave it in front of him and he says, "Turn around, motherfucker, turn around, motherfucker," again with the *MF*.

For some reason, maybe because there are two detectives watching this, a sense of calmness comes over me. Don't ask me why.

He says again, "Turn around." I say, "No, I'm not turning around. Please take the money and go, but I'm not turning around."

(I remember a cop telling me one day, "God forbid you ever get held up, never turn around when being robbed, as they will shoot you in the back and think nothing of it.") I'm thinking to myself, stupidly, *You're going to have to kill me.* I then think and see, as I look in his bloodshot eyes, that he's not got the balls to do it—*you fuckin' coward.* Well, it saved my life that night as the coward grabbed the money and legged it out the door. At this point the two detectives who had witnessed the whole thing run out after him. I subsequently follow after them after I "change my underwear." (Best laxative I've ever had.) When I catch up to them two blocks up, they have the scumbag handcuffed on the street. The two detectives are on top of him, holding him down and waiting for the paddywagon to show up. It shows up seconds later. They ask me if I'm all right, to which I say, "Not sure, think so."

Finally it all hits me—what just happened—and I just slump to the ground in disbelief. Holy shit, did that really just happen?

After I change my underwear *again*, we all go over to the precinct and they arrest that "motherfucker."

On a personal note, God bless the NYPD, because my job as a bartender on the West Side of Manhattan is a lot better because of them. I remember not so long ago all you would get on the street corners here were hookers and drug dealers. Boy, do I miss those days (just kiddin', kinda)—the ugly raw side of the city. But seriously, it is all due to the great work of the NYPD—so cheers, guys.

Wednesday, July 24, 2002
Las Vegas

Had a great week at work—made lots of tips—so I decided to go to Las Vegas. There's no better place to go with a pocket full of cash than Vegas, right, Smithy? We're on the plane flying down to Las Vegas, all excited and looking forward to a few days away, when unfortunately I made a "huge mistake"—I asked the stewardess for the whole can of soda. Whatever you do, don't make the same mistake I did. It's not worth it. I had to sit with my face to the wall for the rest of the flight. She definitely didn't like it when I added, "I'm in the upright and locked position, baby."

This political correctness has gone way too far; it's out of control, for fuck's sake.

I said "stewardess," and she nearly exploded. Her head turned 360 degrees, like in *The Exorcist*, and she shouted, "Well, actually, we are *flight attendants*."

"Sorry," I say. "Why don't ya put the cuckoo back in the clock . . . psycho."

Finally my girlfriend and I arrive in Vegas about 7 p.m. on Saturday night—ready to party. I had just left Manhattan, NYC—party central—but really we are amateurs compared to Vegas. They put on one hell of a show—at least for three days, anyway. Anybody who has been to Las Vegas understands.

What a sight to see, the Vegas strip—but it kinda reminds me of New York. The taxi driver is from Brooklyn, and the first thing he says (in a Brooklyn accent) is, "You know, Vegas is running out of water, so they are going to recycle the toilet water—forgettaboutit!" Now I have two problems with that: number one and number two!

Vegas is all smoke and mirrors, the devil's delight, a middle finger to God with all his trees, rocks, and little bunny rabbits. All that Disney shite. But you know what, it's fantastic.

We find ourselves in the New York-New York Hotel, even though we have just left New York, New York. Walking through the Greenwich Village part of the hotel, not missing the pigeons or the homosexuals. Just kidding, Peter (my lovely gay pal).

We have a great time at the MGM Grand Hotel pool in the daytime and lose all our money at nighttime.

We actually met Howie Mandel, you know, the comedian from the TV show *Deal or No Deal*. I told him that they were actually doing the same show in Africa called *Meal or No Meal*. He laughed and walked away. No handshakes!

I love the slogan they have for Las Vegas; we all know it: "What happens in

Vegas stays in Vegas" (except for herpes—that will come back with ya). I say, "What happens in Vegas you should tell the whole fuckin' world! Tell everyone because it's a mad, brilliant place. But, what happens in the backwoods of a West Virginia farmhouse or a wee shed in Connemara, Galway, Ireland, now that should stay there." (They think the film *Deliverance* is a love story!)

What ya think, Smithy, all those sheep shaggers out there; you know what I'm talking about. Sheep shagging was invented in Ireland. They actually like to do it at the edge of a cliff, as you know, Smithy—gives it a lot more pullback and reminds them of their sister.

Where was I, oh ya, the MGM Grand Hotel in Vegas actually has a swim-up poker table. That's one of many things that makes Vegas "awesome." That means you don't have to leave the game to go to the bathroom. Remember what they say: "What happens in a Vegas pool stays in a Vegas pool."

Cheers for now, and please tip your bartender, especially this broke-arse one. Remember, I just got back from Vegas—talk soon.

TWELVE

Thursday, August 1, 2002
Who Are You?

Wait until I tell you what happened to me last night, Smithy. This is a good one. The bar is packed, as it normally is when there's a concert in Madison Square Garden. I'm running around like a blue-arsed fly serving all The Who fans who are packing in before they head over to the concert. I really enjoy these nights, particularly when it's one of my favorite bands playing in concert. Everything is going well, customers are served, and The Who is blaring out of the bar's jukebox—life is grand.

I notice this rather large man squeeze his way through the crowd and up to the bar. He asks me for a bottle of Heineken, pays me, and gives me a twenty-dollar tip. "Let me know when a seat at the bar comes available." I say, "I've got one at the end of the bar," and I tell one of my friends to "fuck off for a minute and let my new friend sit down." We start talking and right away I like this man. It usually always helps when you start with a twenty-dollar tip. In between serving, we chat about football and music. As the bar starts to slow down, we get to talk more, and he tells me his name is "Rex King" and that he is the tour manager for The Who. He asks me if I would like to go to the concert tonight. "Fuck, I would love to go, but I'm working tonight. Can't get out," I say. He says, "How about Sunday night? They are playing again then." "Sure, I would love it; I'm off Sunday night." I give him my number and he tells me that he will call me the next day.

Smithy, you know how much I love The Who, right? Well, like most things I don't expect a call the next day, but when he does call me, it makes it that much sweeter. He says, "Hey, it's Rex. I have two tickets for you, but the only thing is, you will have to pick them up in the Rihga Royal Hotel on Fifty-Fourth Street between Sixth and Seventh Avenues." "No worries," I say. "Are you kidding me? That's brilliant." I run up to the hotel like a lunatic, just in case there's some kind of mistake or he changes his mind. The receptionist tells me to wait as somebody is coming down with the tickets. Next thing I see Zak Starkey, Ringo Starr's son, walking toward me saying, in a very British accent, "'Ere ya go, mate, enjoy the show," and hands me an envelope with two tickets and two backstage passes in it. Zak is the drummer for The Who. I shake his hand, thank him, and tell him I will see him later, then run out the door. Well, Michelle and I head off excitedly to the Garden. We enter the Garden and the usher keeps walking us closer and closer to the stage until we are practically on it. We can't believe it. We are almost on the stage—front row, side of the stage. Sitting behind us are Bruce Springsteen, Stevie Van Zandt, Sting, and some of the coolest rockers on the planet. I guess The Who brings them all out!

Well, they come on stage, practically walking past us, and the crowd in the Garden erupts—goes fuckin' bananas. I can still feel it and hear it now. They start with the song "Who Are You." We look around, and we are the only two people standing up in our section—I suppose they are all way too cool to stand up. Actually they totally fuckin' are. In between one of their songs, Pete Townsend points over to Michelle and me and says, "Look at those two groovy people dancing." We look around to make sure it's us that he is referring to, then we stare at each other (as the Garden crowd roars), and we just start screaming like two little girls. Well, I did.

Then he jams into the classic song "Baba O'Reilly." What an experience, with the whole Garden crowd roaring. Smithy, it gets even better. The concert ends and now we are heading backstage to hopefully meet the band. We're like Wayne and Garth in the classic Mike Myers film *Wayne's World*—showing our backstage passes to everybody. Sure enough, they're all there, and they couldn't have been nicer. Mind you, I couldn't understand a fuckin' word Roger Daltrey said, but he sure sings incredibly well. I see Rex, the tour manager, backstage, and before we know it, we're all at this bar beside their hotel until we then find ourselves back at Zak Starkey's hotel room partying literally like "rock stars."

We leave at 8 a.m. or so the following morning—walk out the entrance of the Rihga Royal Hotel just as the sun is peeking through the skyline of New York City. Michelle and I just look at each other in total amazement, and we say at the exact same time, "Did that really just happen?"

What a night, Smithy. What a bleedin' night—a night I will never forget.

Tuesday, January 14, 2003
Psychiatrist versus Bartender

Quiet night at the bar last night. Spent most of the night chatting with my mate Dave. He's quite the character, as are most people from Liverpool, England. Well as I said, it was pretty slow, so we had time to talk about many things, from football (the *real* football, you know, the one where you actually use your foot—hence, the name), to personal fears and so on. He starts telling me his fear of thinking that there's someone or something under his bed. It went something like this:

Ever since I was a child, I've always had a fear of someone under my bed at night. So I went to a shrink and told him, "I've got problems. Every time I go to bed I think there's somebody under it. I'm scared. I think I'm going crazy."

"Just put yourself in my hands for one year," said the shrink. "Come talk to me three times a week, and we should be able to get rid of those fears."

"How much do you charge?"

"Ninety dollars per visit," replied the doctor.

"I'll sleep on it," I said.

Six months later the doctor met me on the street.

"Why didn't you ever come to see me about those fears you were having?" he asked.

"Well, ninety bucks a visit, three times a week for a year, is an awful lot of money! My friend the bartender cured me for ten dollars. I was so happy to have saved all that money that I went out and bought myself a new custom-fitted suit!"

"Is that so?" With a bit of an attitude, he said, "And how, may I ask, did a *bartender* cure you?"

"He told me to cut the legs off the bed! Ain't nobody under there now!"

Apparently I gave my good friend Dave that advice six months ago—who knew I was so brilliant?

So go have a drink and talk to your bartender! Life is too short!

And remember to always tip your bartender! They are a lot cheaper than a shrink!

Saturday, April 5, 2003
Another Funny Bar Story

My two friends Tony and Steve are telling me this story at the bar one day. I've gotta share this with ya, Smithy.

Tony and Steve are getting very drunk at the bar when suddenly Steve throws up all over himself. "Oh no, now my wife will kill me," he says. Tony says, "Don't worry, pal, just tuck a twenty-dollar bill in your breast pocket and tell Jane that someone threw up on you and gave you twenty dollars for the dry cleaning bill."

So they stay for another couple of hours and get even drunker. Eventually Steve rolls into his house and his wife, Jane, starts screaming at him. "You reek of alcohol and you've puked all over yourself. My God, you're disgusting."

Speaking very carefully so as not to slur, Steve says, "Nowainaminit, I can e'splain everythin! Itsh snot wha jew think, I only had a cupla drrrinks, but thiss other guy got ssick on me . . . he had one too many and he juss couldin hold hizz liguor, he said he was verrry sorry an' gave me twennie dollars for the cleaning bill!"

Jane looks in the breast pocket and says, "But this is forty dollars."

"Oh yeah . . . I almos' fergot, he shhhit in my pants, too."

Saturday, July 19, 2003
The Bar Loser

Working in a popular bar, you always have a "Bar Loser." If you don't know what or whom I'm talking about, you are that loser. You know, the person who always makes excuses about everything. The person who can never pay his tab or bar bill in full—ever. He's always saying, "Here's twenty dollars; take that off my tab." Like Norm from *Cheers*. He always has a sure thing at the bookies. Comes into the bar with the horse-racing part of the paper under his arm and the bookies' pencil behind his ear. When he goes to the track, the teller gives him his ticket already torn up.

What I've noticed from working behind the bar is the difference between alcoholics and junkies. An alcoholic will steal your wallet and actually feel guilty about it, whereas a junkie will steal your wallet and then help you look for it.

I hate when people come into the bar and look at me like I'm speaking

Chinese when I say, "Hi, what can I get you?" If I spoke Chinese I would have found Nina—remember? People, what do you think I just asked you? You came into a bar, I'm the bartender behind the bar, and I say something. I wonder what I could possibly be saying. Tell me what you want so I can move on and get another drink for someone else, nob head. Thanks a lot.

Some people must think the bar is in a lighthouse. I got a call the other night and the person said to me, "Is the coast clear?" That's weird, right? Other people must think I sell drugs because the other night I got a call and the person on the phone said to me, "Is that dope gone yet?" You must be really drunk when you get pulled over by the Coast Guard.

This Afghanistan man came into the bar and asked me if I could recommend a good port. I said, "Yup, Newark, New Jersey. Piss off!"

Anyway, I'm working behind the bar the other evening—pretty dead—when in walks this man. All that he is wearing is a hospital gown—arse hanging out for the whole world to see, name tag on his wrist, and no shoes. (Sounds like the start of a joke, right?) It's no joke. Well, he walks up to the bar, calmly sits down, and asks me for a pint of Bud Light. How's he going to pay for it? Not like he has a wallet on him or anything. If he does, hate to think where it is. I look at him and ask, "You okay? Do you need some help?" Remember, all he is wearing is a hospital gown. He looks me right in the eye and softly says, "Yes, I do." He goes on to tell me that he has just walked out of Bellevue Hospital, got on the M34 crosstown bus, and got off at Thirty-Fourth and Ninth Avenue. I mean, where do you start? How could he just walk out of a "mental" hospital, get on a bus, and end up in my bar without anybody calling the police or doing anything for this poor man? I tell him, "Why don't we walk up to the Midtown South Police Station and they can help you? Would you like that?" He says again, in a very matter-of-fact, soft voice, "Thanks, I would like that." We walk up the street, me holding this half-naked man's hand, and I bring him in the police station to the surprise of everyone there. Only in New York is a half-naked man wearing a hospital gown on a bus and walking in the street not unusual, Smithy!

Wednesday, August 6, 2003
From Russia with Love

Well, Smithy, I arrived at work tonight to find this gorgeous waitress from Russia working at the restaurant. What a sight to see—better than that ugly wagon (God bless her) we hired at the start of the summer. Summers are quiet.

A face on her like a kicked-in can of Pedigree Chum. A face only a mother could love—not even sure if her mother could love it, unless she was blind. She was lucky if people would sell her magazines.

Once in a while a customer will date one of the waitresses. It's usually a bad idea, and I've yet to see it end well. It's okay for me, of course!

What happens is, when the relationship sours, and they ultimately always do, the customer avoids the bar like the plague! And if he has any friends, he starts to arrange to meet them in different places, and you end up losing a customer and, more importantly, customers. Or worse yet, they'll haunt the place, stalking their prey until you have to throw them out for good. I've experienced many a Romeo's attempt to memorize the schedules of their exes. They actually end up being there more than the waitress. I had one bloke who would show up when one of the waitresses was supposed to already be there, and so I would always know who was working that night.

One man even made off with a Xeroxed copy of the schedule. I've seen lads stand across the street, waiting for them. "Oh, hey there, just happened to be walking by."

I had one customer leave her bra and knickers (panties) on the bar for me. They can be great tips, but unfortunately cash tips are generally better!

I had another girl from New Jersey who wanted to date me. What a bloody nerve. Go to New Jersey? You must be fuckin' kiddin' me. Go through that sewer that you call the Holland Tunnel and flush yourself back to New Jersey. I have done a lot of things to get a ride, but I'm not going to that kip you call New Jersey.

Anyway, this new Russian waitress is a fuckin' stunner. Needless to say, I've got an instant one on me. She's so hot that you should call your doctor if you don't have a hard-on for more than four hours. You should hear the way she talks to the customers—in typical Russian stereotype. "You giff me tip now." She even ran after a customer tonight because he didn't give her the appropriate tip that she required. I'm sure all the charm schools in Russia are pretty empty. Smithy, she is a fuckin' delight to watch. She gets away with it; it's a thing of beauty, and a fuckin' work of art. I think I'm in love. It's funny, but the Russian language has a way of making any simple request sound like an air-raid warning.

Now it's the end of the night, and me, Katrina Kirilenko—the Russian wrecking ball (Miss Stalin)—and Ray, one of the regulars, are sitting down drinking. Ray suggests we go to his mate's bar on Spring and Greenwich Street. We all leave the bar, and they get into a taxi outside. I lock up the bar and open the side door of the taxi where Katrina is sitting and sort of, like, indicate for her to scooch over. She just looks at me, stone-faced cold, like

I'm some kind of an insect that she could step on and crush. So I ended up sitting in the front seat beside the driver, to the disappointment of both of us. I turn around, trying to chat with Katrina, as we're driving down Ninth Avenue toward Greenwich Street. I ask her where exactly in Russia she is from, and she says, "Severomorsk," like she could have been telling me to go fuck myself, and then she goes back to fiddling about with her phone. I look over at Ray, and he's just smiling as he stares out the window of the taxi. We stop at the Ear Inn, and Ray and I go in for a few scoops and leave Katrina—you guessed it, Smithy—outside playing on her phone. Then all of a sudden, we hear the *clop, clop, clop* of her high-heeled boots and turn to see her coming into the bar, her walk as cool and confident as a catwalk model! Everybody turns to see her, and once they see her, the whole bar couldn't take their eyes off her. She was, like I said, Smithy, a sight worth seeing. Everybody—men and women—just sat in total fuckin' awe (especially me) as this magnificent creature walked, all sexy and sultry, full of confidence, toward Ray and me. Fuckin' excellent!

We all start knocking back shots of vodka, and now we're all getting nice and pissed. We drink copious amounts of vodka. It's like water to her. I'm fuckin' twisted. She's telling us how she used to be in the Russian army and how she barely escaped with her life. I'm even more in love with her now.

Well, it's time to go, and we're back in a taxi doing it all over again, except this time I'm in the back and Ray's in the front. We drop Ray off, and now it's time to drop Katrina off. We pull up outside her apartment, up the street from Ray's, and she doesn't even say good night; she just jumps up and walks out of the taxi. She's as cold as a prostitute's tit in Siberia. I wait with the door still open to make sure she gets into her apartment okay. Really, I wouldn't fuck with this girl. I see her get her keys out of her twenty-dollar knockoff Gucci handbag that she got in Chinatown. Turns the lock in the door and opens it. I reach and go to close the taxi door when Katrina turns around and says to me, "Well, harr you fugging cummin in?"

I know Mick had told me, "Don't fuck the waitresses," but come on, Smithy, with an invitation like that, I certainly couldn't pass it up!

I see her the next night at work, and she's back to being Miss Stalin—actually, that's fine with me, to be honest with ya, Smithy; less drama that way. But I'll tell you one thing, she makes Stalin look like an altar boy.

Talk to you soon, mate.

THIRTEEN

Thursday, August 14, 2003
The Blackout

I'm sure you heard that the lights went out in New York City—actually, most of the northeast of America. I'm sitting in my apartment on Ninth Avenue, drinking coffee, listening to some music, when all of a sudden the music and lights go out. It's about four o'clock in the afternoon. Now this is pretty standard in this kip and building I live in, so I wasn't that concerned. Then I get a call on my cell phone from my mate Dave. He is down in Florida, and it's all over the news how the lights have gone out in the northeast part of America, and at this point they don't know why. Now all of a sudden, the noise starts to slowly rise outside my bedroom window, which as you know, faces onto the very busy Ninth Avenue. I start to think all the bad thoughts, particularly so soon after 9/11. I'm sure I'm not the only one. I look out the window from the third floor as I start to walk out onto the fire escape, and I see all the traffic lights are out and the traffic is starting to build up, and confusion is setting in. I see Louie the cop directing traffic on Thirty-Fifth Street, and I shout down to him, "What happened?" He says, "There was some kind of an electrical outage up in Canada that caused the power grid to shut down." "That's it, Louie?" I say. "Nothing serious to worry about?" He confirms that everything will be fine. I trust Louie, as I know him very well from the bar, and if he says everything will be fine, then everything will be fine.

I get to work at six o'clock and the bar is jam-packed. What adds to the fun is that it is a sunny, very hot summer's night. Not only is the bar packed inside, it's also jammers outside on the street. It's actually one of the busiest nights I've ever worked behind the bar to date. As the daytime turns into night, it gets interesting. We have already put candles out and gone next door to the hardware store for extra batteries for the torches—so we are well prepared. What a fun night it turns out to be. We sell out of pretty much every beer we have.

We are lucky because we have a lot of beers on ice, so they all stay cold—well, cool anyway. It's funny how people get excited when the lights go out. I think it reminds us of when we were young, and we just turn into kids again.

Here's where the real fun begins. It's now four o'clock in the morning, not one problem in the bar or out on the street. Considering all the lights are out, this is quite remarkable. I know when the lights went out in NYC in 1977, things were a lot different—there were actually riots all over the city. It's a credit to the cops, and maybe because it was pretty close after 9/11, everybody seemed to just come together and help. Sure, half the bar was staying in my apartment that night as all public transportation had been canceled. I'm sure there will be a baby boom in about nine months. My friend John the detective is at the end of the bar, and everyone else has gone home or up to my place. I say to John, "I'm out of here. I'm going to walk up to Times Square to see how it looks in the dark. Let's go." John says, "I'll drive and you bring some beers." "Sounds good."

What a sight to see as we drive through Times Square in his unmarked police car. It's pretty much in the dark except for a few generator lights and some news crews. John flashes his badge, and we drive straight through and across Forty-Second Street to Grand Central. Here people are sleeping on the streets outside of the hotels on each side of the street. The hotels have to have their guests out of the hotels when the power is out. It's an incredible sight. We drive down the FDR Drive, which goes north and south along the east side of Manhattan and along the East River. John and I are having a grand party, and while we're driving he points out the various bridges that span across the East River connecting Manhattan with Queens and Brooklyn. He tells me how to remember the bridges, starting with the Brooklyn Bridge going north to the Manhattan Bridge and on to the Williamsburg Bridge, which all connect lower Manhattan to Brooklyn. "Just think of the car," he says, "BMW—Brooklyn, Manhattan, and Williamsburg Bridges." "Cool, and I will never forget that"—thanks, John. As we're driving and partying, I notice John is starting to sway a wee bit in the car. I say, "Pull over and let me drive. I've been working all night, I'm fine." Knowing he now shouldn't be driving, John gets into the passenger seat and lets me drive. Now I'm driving John's unmarked police car through lower Manhattan. Who knew that one day I would be living in NYC and driving an unmarked police car?

We chat a bit more, pick up some beers, and even stop off at this after-hours bar I know on Barrow Street. Eventually we head back to Midtown South and I park his car on Thirty-Fifth Street at about eight in the morning. Thanks a lot, John, for the tour and the great night.

FOURTEEN

This is for all the bartenders—the people who eat their dinner standing up, and the people who have a great job but have to put up with wankers once in a while. We bartenders know the people—the ones who come into bars and ask for extra liquor or say, "I can't taste the liquor in this Long Island iced tea or martini," or (by the way, there are going to be a lot of *ors*), "Can I have it with no ice?" or, "Straight up with coke on the side?" or, "Hook me up!" That's the best line—"Hook me up!"—but they fail every time to hook up the bartender.

When will "these people" get it—you get nothing for nothing, especially when you don't tip. Bartenders and most people know the people I am talking about. The people who want everything and give zero in return. Slavery was abolished many moons ago—let it go. I love the verbal tip—the one where they say how wonderful everything was and then walk out the fucking door. Even better when people say, "I would like a greyhound" (which is just vodka and grapefruit juice). Oh, it's so hard to say "vodka and grapefruit." What are you too fuckin' cool to ask for a vodka and grapefruit? Dickhead. I always charge these fucking snobs more. I usually say, "The pet shop is up the block; this is a bar, douchebag." I had this girl come in and say, "Can I have a *cuba libre*?" which I found out is simply a rum and Coke. Now, I have been bartending for many years now, and I have never heard of a rum and Coke being referred to as anything but a rum and Coke. Would you get over yourself and get a fuckin' life? It's a rum and Coke; it's not a *cuba libre*—that's some place in Cuba where some of us are not allowed to go. Hope you're allowed to go, Miss *Cuba Libre*. Why don't you go and stay the fuck there, you pretentious twat?

I had these three people come into the bar the other night, and they were questioning the price of the drinks, as all these cunts do. If you have to question the price of the drink, stay the fuck home, you oxygen wasters.

Anyway, they are questioning the price of the drink and I tell them it's the price and that's it. They do this purposely so as to make them feel okay about leaving no tip. So they leave me five cents as a tip; remember the headline: I don't like to *hear* my tip. So a couple of days go by and I see these big tippers in the bar again. I get five cents out of the register and give it back to the people and say, "You left this here last week. Do you want change?" Remember, for every action there is always a reaction. Well, they say to me that I was so rude. "Rude?" I say. "I'm not the one leaving five-cent tips. Go fuck yourself." I guess I'm becoming a New Yorker, as I'm starting to sound like that guy whom I asked for directions the first day I landed in New York. Ah well.

Talking about tipping, this man comes into the bar and says to me, "What's the biggest tip you ever got?" I think about it for a second and say, "A hundred dollars." He gives me two hundred dollars. Then he says, "Who was the guy that gave you the tip? Maybe I might know him." I say, "Yes, it was you."

I like to keep my stories funny because that's what I'm really interested in, so I want to tell you a funny story I heard.

This man was telling me this story the other night and I thought it was so funny.

He leaves my bar one night, and at the end of the street you have the Cheyenne Diner on Thirty-Third Street and Ninth Avenue. Outside this diner there is a taxi stand, so a lot of taxi drivers park outside to go to the diner. This guy jumps into a taxi with the keys in it, obviously fucked-up drunk, and somehow makes it home to Sunnyside, Queens. Well, he wakes up the next morning all hungover and feeling lousy. His wife is all pissed off at him for coming home late and drunk. She says to him, "I hope you didn't drive home at least; I hope you got a taxi home." He says nothing for a second, puts his head out the window of his apartment, and says, "Of course I did. I got a taxi home." And the taxi he stole a few hours before is still outside his door. He swears it's a true story, Smithy.

Saturday, November 1, 2003
Ways to Get a Bartender's Attention and Keep It!

Catch his eye—a bartender is always looking up to see who needs what—and then gesture. Don't yell, snap your fingers, or whistle; he's not a dog—good luck getting a drink after that! I had this one shithead whistle at me one night. I said, "Is there a dog in here?" Then I left to look for it and never came back to the dog whistler.

Know what you want to drink before the bartender asks. If you're ordering for other people, also know what they want. There's nothing worse than when you're busy and you ask somebody what you can get him or her and they look at you with a blank look on their face. Why don't you call me up tomorrow and I'll tell you what shoes to wear. Make a fuckin' decision, will ya?

If you're ordering for other people, please have everyone's money in hand, ready to pay, so the bartender doesn't have to wait, and don't be a cheap prick—leave a nice tip. The less time you take, the more time I have to serve others and make more tips. It's a numbers game.

If you want a specific brand, ask for it by name. If you ask me for a vodka and cranberry, you're getting the cheap bar vodka. Don't tell me after I make it that you wanted Grey Goose vodka.

If you know you'll be coming back for another round and you're paying with a credit card, leave the tab open so the bartender doesn't have to run through new charges when you return.

Believe me, if you do these things, the bartender will remember you, you will get served right away, and he might even buy you a drink or a round. If the bartender is good, next time you come up to the bar you will just have to say "same again," and he will give you the same round again.

How to Tip Appropriately!

One dollar a drink is fine. If you're running a tab, leave 20 percent of the total, as you would if you were dining.

Don't tell the bartender you'll "get him later." What that means to him is you will "get him never," and he'll be slower to come back to you when you want your next round—or he might never come back.

If a bartender finds you attractive, he may give you a free drink. You should still tip him, even if the house isn't charging you.

Don't punish the bartender because you think the drinks are too expensive. He didn't set the price, and you've chosen to drink them. Nobody got rich stiffing bartenders and not tipping.

Please don't leave loose change on the bar as a tip. Round up in dollar increments. Bartenders don't like to hear their tips.

The other night in the bar, this prick kept asking me for a buyback—a free drink. In most NYC bars they will give you a free drink, usually after you have had three drinks or more. However, it is up to the discretion of the bar and the bartender. Anyway, this guy says to me, "Where's my free drink?" When you ask for one, you don't get one. That's what I believe. So I say, "We don't give free drinks here." This cunt keeps asking me, "Where's my free drink, my buyback?" "We don't give free drinks," I continue to say. Now this loser starts shouting, "Where's my fuckin' free drink? I'm going to kick your fuckin' ass, motherfucker." So I give him ten dollars and say, "Go and buy yourself a drink somewhere else and fuck off and don't come back, ya wanker." He says, "Thanks a lot," and leaves the bar. Sometimes it's worth a few dollars to get rid of a scumbag prick.

Things not to say to a bartender when they're busy: "Would you recommend a nice fruity drink?" Yes, a bottle of Bud. Now fuck off!

Speaking of tipping, tourists—here's the deal: We bartenders make our living on tips; it is customary to tip in America, especially in New York City, and if you don't tip it is also customary to spit in your margarita. You will be getting a saliva colada tonight.

Here's the deal: We live on the tips, so give a few dollars for a round of drinks; most New Yorkers give a dollar a drink. I know this is all new to you, so give what you can. Anything is appreciated, and it is also customary to buy a customer a drink, especially one who tips, usually every fourth drink. I know this is a revolutionary idea to you Europeans right now, as you are lucky to get a free bag of bacon fries from your local bar at home. Don't wait until the end of the night to tip; show your appreciation right away, and the appreciation will be shown to you. One last thing: what is it with people wanting to split a check after they have had one drink each, and then wanting to put it on two separate credit cards? What did you just meet each other outside the bar? Come on, for fuck's sake—you obviously know each other. Here's a crazy idea: why don't one of you pick up the sixteen-dollar check and then the other person pick up the next one? Or better again, why don't you take twenty dollars out of your purse or wallet and pay the bleedin' check with cash! Also, I love it when people's credit cards are declined. I run the card, it's declined by the credit card company, and people act so surprised. "Oh my God, I can't believe it! How could my credit card be declined? There must be some mistake? I have thousands of dollars in that account." No, you don't, pal. You're a deadbeat who doesn't pay his bills. Don't get so surprised; you know exactly what's going on.

I know, Smithy, I usually end off my letters by saying "don't forget to tip your bartender," but we have to stop this tipping people for counter service. No one should get a tip for standing upright, moving a few feet to the left or right, and picking up a muffin. Save your cash tips for bartenders—give the others the change! I'm sorry. Cheers, mate.

Tuesday, December 9, 2003
Webster Apartments

I meet a lot of girls in the bar from the local all-girls housing around the corner. Wish I could get an apartment in there! They're all very nice and cute—well, the ones I've met so far anyway. I'm talking to one of the residents at the bar, and she explains that the building was originally owned by Macy's, for all the women workers. It is now for workingwomen in the city who make below a certain amount each week. Beth from England pays two hundred dollars a week, and that includes room and board and two meals a day. Before we know it, its four o'clock in the morning, we are loaded drunk, and it is time for me and Beth to go home—I hope anyway. We walk around the corner to the Skylight Diner and have a beer and some breakfast. Then a bunch of her friends come in and join us. We all finish up and we walk across the street to the Webster Apartments, where she lives. Now I'm intrigued after she has told me all about the apartments. I ask her, "Can you show me the apartment?" It's at this point that I learn the "rules" about Webster Apartments. She informs me that men are not allowed to stay over and they have to be off the premises by ten o'clock at night. They can have men over for dinner—we're having dinner tomorrow night.

Well, I'm sitting having dinner with Beth, surrounded by about one hundred women. I think there are maybe two other lads in the room. I notice one of the other lads and we kinda give each other the ceremonial "what's up, dude" look, thinking we are as cool as shite. We've died and gone to heaven. It's kinda like having dinner in a women's prison—for fuck's sake, it's brilliant. The food, I would imagine, is also like being in prison!

Anyway, Beth comes in late the next night with a few of her friends. They are all well oiled and feeling no pain, giggling away. We have a few shots, and the girls have the best idea ever. "Let's smuggle you into the apartments tonight." Always up for a good caper, I agree. Here's what we do: I wear one of their hats and coats and just walk right into the women's prison surrounded by them, right in the middle of them so the night watchman (prison guard) can't see me. "Sure, he's always half asleep anyway," the girls say. Brilliant. This is so hot and exciting. Her room is small; the bed is about the size of a fish finger, and there's a sink in the corner. Before we know it, the sun is coming up, and it's now time for me to "break out." We didn't really think this through, and now it's time to figure out the great escape.

The great escape didn't quite turn out to be so great. I get in the elevator on the twelfth floor, and as Murphy's Law goes, the elevator seems to stop on every floor. Each time a few girls get in. I'm trying to hide in the corner with my head down so as not to get any eye contact and not draw too much attention to myself. It's kinda impossible, considering it's an all-girls building and I'm the only fella in the elevator. It is pretty tough considering the situation. "Don't pay any attention to the male elephant in the elevator!" It seems to last forever, but eventually the elevator stops on the ground floor. The elevator is now full, which works in my flavor. I walk out again in the middle of a crowd of girls and walk briskly for the door. I never looked back. Sometimes you just gotta put your head down and leg it. All I could hear were the fading sounds of the doorman: "Excuse me, excuse me, excuse me!" Before the fella at the desk knew what was going on, I was halfway across Thirty-Fourth Street.

Monday, December 29, 2003
I've Got to Get Another Job!

This man walks into the bar and asks me for a gin and tonic. I make it for him, and when I return with his change, he is already finished. "Give me another one," he says. I have a bad feeling in my gut about this one. Trying to lighten up things a little, I say, "Boy, you sure are thirsty." He says again, "Just give me another one." I can see he is sweating and he looks like he's on something. He should not be sweating considering it's cold outside—it's December in New York City. I walk away to serve a few more people when I hear him again slurping the end of his drink through the straw. "Give me another one." I say, "Relax; take it easy on them drinks." He says, "Don't tell me to take it easy; just give me another drink." I say, "It's my job to look out for people, so relax, and I will give you another one in a bit," as I walk away to the other end of the bar. I go back to him in about ten minutes, and I can see he's not happy. He unbuttons his suit jacket and opens up one side of it to reveal a gun, then he says, "If you don't make me another drink, I will shoot you." I make him another drink and say, "Cheers, it's on the house." He sucks it down again, says "thank you," smiles, and walks right out the door. For fuck's sake, Smithy, I've got to get another job!

Let's hope I never see this fucker again.

Working behind the bar   Look closely—The Irish Curse . . . my arse!

Behind the bar

Caricature of me by Kate,
a customer from the bar

FIFTEEN

Friday, January 2, 2004
Happy New Year to All

Well, New Year's Eve was quite a night at the bar—crazy busy, but as usual, a lot of fun. Thanks to all who came out, except for a few. You know who you are—wankers. A special thanks to all my friends and family who made it extra-special; I really enjoyed our champagne toast at midnight. Cheers, and have a fun and healthy 2004!

One person actually gave me a twenty-dollar bill when I asked him for ID. I'm like, "You don't look anything like Andrew Jackson, but you could look like Franklin. Check your money later?" Another guy comes in and his breath nearly knocked me over. It came straight from Satan's arse. I said, "How about you brush your teeth next year? Now that's a New Year's resolution."

These prostitutes come into the bar late. I know them—one is named Pepsi. I have affection for them, as they are always very nice and respectful. My partner at the bar asks me, "Do they have ID?" I say to him, "Prostitutes don't carry ID—they usually carry VD."

I just read an article in *The New York Times* on the dangers of drinking alcohol. That's it; my New Year's resolution is to stop reading.

Here's one I heard at the bar, Smithy. What do you think? Three men die on Christmas Eve, and to get into heaven, Saint Peter says, "You must have something on you that represents Christmas." The Englishman flicks on his cigarette lighter and says, "It's a candle." Saint Peter lets him pass. A Welshman pulls out a set of keys, jingles them, and says, "They are bells." Saint Peter lets him pass. And then an Irishman pulls out a G-string and Saint Peter says, "How the fuck do they represent Christmas?"

The Irishman says, "They're Carol's!" Saint Peter smiles and lets him in.

So here's to a prosperous New Year, and please remember, always tip your bartender.

Sunday, February 22, 2004
Central Park: The Eighth Wonder of the World?

Being a bartender in New York City is amazing. It's the most fun you can have with your trousers on—sometimes off. I will continue to do it until I stop enjoying it. However, like every job there are times when it's difficult and stressful. When the job gets a wee bit stressful, I love to go to Central Park, in the heart of Manhattan. If it's only for an hour once in a while, for me it's like a mini-holiday. It's my NYC shrink, and it costs a lot less. A big couch in the middle of the city, Central Park is the heart that beats New York City for me. The sixth borough. Manhattan and Central Park are the only places I know where you can be truly alone. When I tell people that, they have a hard time understanding it, but when you live here you will understand. Even with so many people in this city, it is a place where people do their own thing and mind their own business. I like that. I love to run, and for me there is no place like Central Park. The greens of the Great Lawn, the calmness amidst the reservoir, or simply running the six-mile track inside the park are perfect.

Once you enter, everything slows down and gets so peaceful. It's no wonder Yoko Ono put the spiritual tribute to John Lennon (Strawberry Fields) in Central Park. The energy is high yet tranquil. The excitement and anticipation of peace and quiet pulls you in. The park is over 150 years old, over 80 percent of it is below street level, it's over 800 acres, it's the first public park built in America, and the perimeter is over six miles long, from Fifty-Ninth Street to 110th Street.

There are so many points of interest, I could not possibly mention them all, and to be honest with ya, I don't want to share them all, as I want them all to myself. But here are a few:

Go see John over by the Plaza at Fifty-Ninth Street on the southeast corner of the park. He is a real character. Look for him and Romeo—his white and black spotted horse. Take a ride with him on his horse and carriage; he's full of fascinating information and stories. Ask him about David Beckham, Tom Cruise, and Al Pacino, just to name a few.

Small villages made up mostly of German, black, and Irish once occupied Central Park. If you enter the park on the southeast corner on Fifth Avenue (where John is, by the Plaza Hotel), as you go down the steps to the park and the pond, there is a German light post that was dedicated to the German village that was once there. Up by the National Museum of History around Eightieth Street and CPW, there is a black statue that is dedicated to the black village that was once there. And if you enter the park at the Columbus Circle entrance at Fifty-Ninth Street and CPW, where the Irish village once was, there is a banjo and a couple of empty bottles of whiskey.

There's actually a Scottish man who always plays his bagpipes just south of the Metropolitan Museum at Eighty-Second Street in the park—sporting his kilt and all. He sounds great. There's nothing quite like the sound of the bagpipes. Once you hear them in the park, particularly when the sun is going down, it's remarkable and haunting. Always reminds me of my Scottish pal Stevie.

At Seventy-Second Street and Central Park South it is always nice to stop by Strawberry Fields and relax by the IMAGINE sign that was put there in honor of the late, great John Lennon, who was tragically shot across the street outside of the Dakota Building where Yoko Ono still lives. What's yellow, small, ugly, smells of urine, and sleeps alone? Yoko Ono. Oh, that's mean!

Then head down to Heckscher Ballfields at West Sixty-Third Street, bring a sandwich, and look for Smokey; he will get you a beer to wash down your lunch. In the summertime there are continuous baseball and softball games there. Lots of free entertainment. Many workers from the local Broadway shows. A great place to relax, have a beer, and take it all in. I think a lot of New Yorkers take Central Park for granted and forget how beautiful the park really is. Oh the simple things in life.

That's enough for now. And when you're finished in the park, come down to my bar. Don't forget to give me a tip, especially now after all this great information. Cheers, and you're welcome!

Monday, April 5, 2004
Hockey

New York Rangers in the Garden tonight. Always a busy, entertaining night when they play! The fans are terrific. They usually start coming in a few hours before the game and have a few beers and a bite to eat before heading off for the fight. Pleasure to serve. There's an old joke: "I went to a boxing match, and a hockey game broke out." I've gone to a few games over the years and met some of the players. They are very down-to-earth and fun to be around. I remember one night this fella was annoying this girl at the bar. You know, one of these morons who keeps talking to the girl even though she is reading a book and obviously doesn't want anything to do with this jackass. He says something to her, she looks up and says, "Really," then turns around and goes back to reading her book. Well, I say, "Listen, mate, do me a favor and leave the girl alone. Just drink your beer, okay?" As always this fuckhead now gets the lump with me. You can never win in these situations. "Fuck you," he says to me. "Alright, now you're out." As he's leaving, he says to me, "Why don't you tell me that outside?" He's leaving so that's all I care about. Heard it many times before. The best thing to do is to say nothing and let him have his last word. Give him his victory. He's leaving, after all. I say to myself, "Ya, if I'm not there in time, start without me."

Ninety percent of the time they usually just go—but not this mindless fucker! He starts banging on the window, raising his fist, saying, "Come out here and tell me to leave." The customers at the bar, mostly hockey fans, are all saying to me, "You want me to handle this?" They're queuing up. "No, just ignore him; he'll go away." I know what hockey fans are like; they will just go out there and lay him out.

"Bang, bang." He's still out banging on the window. Now he comes into the bar shouting, "Fuck you, bartender, come outside and tell me to leave."

Why would I go outside to tell him to leave when he's already outside? Before I know it, one of the hockey fans goes outside, and *bam*, it's all over. He's out cold, sprawled out in the rubbish on the side of the street. The hockey fan comes back in and continues to eat his burger like nothing happened. He looks up with a mouth full of meat. "Ssoorry, hee waass annoyyiinng mee." I look over his shoulder out the window to see the lad picking himself up and stumbling down the street. Some people just don't know when to quit.

Anyway, it's about eleven o'clock, and the game is over as a few fans start to come in. Some of them have come just to take a piss. Then my good friend the ex-Rangers player comes in. He is now retired and works hospitality for the Rangers. Whenever I see him, I know I'm going to lose all the tips I've made so far in the night. We usually play poker—actually, the game is called liars poker. He's a good tipper, so I don't mind so much, and he has treated me to a bunch of hockey games over the years. He's a great lad, actually. You would think an Irishman like myself would be good at a game where the main ingredient is lying. After all, we're pretty good fibbers.

Basically, Smithy, you use the serial numbers on the dollar bills like playing cards. You bluff (lie) about the amount of numbers you and the other players might have. About an hour passes, and I'm already down about a hundred dollars. The bar is now pretty quiet, when in walk Mark Messier and Eric Lindros. Big fuckers, too, especially Lindros! Now the four of us are playing. I'm playing liars poker with three legends of hockey. Twelve Stanley Cups between them all. That's the biggest cup and honor you can win in hockey. It's probably equivalent to winning the Premier League or FA Cup in England. We're having a few beers, playing away, when Lindros says, "Let's play for hundreds," as he takes out a wad of bills from his pocket. "Okay," the others collectively say as they turn to look at me. "Sorry, lads, that's too rich for me." Then they all start to laugh. Messier says, "No, you stay in for a dollar."

Smithy, what this meant was that every time I lost, I owed the pot three dollars, but every time one of them lost, they owed three hundred dollars. "Grand! Thanks a lot," I say. "I'm back in." Very classy!

End of the night, I'm up two thousand seven hundred dollars. "Thanks for coming in; the drinks are on me." They can come back anytime—legends on and off the ice. Let's go, Rangers!

Saturday, July 24, 2004
Cheese!

I love when people at the bar ask me, "Can you take a photo?" We all know the power of a photo and the memories they capture, so I'm always happy to take a picture—well, usually anyway. Everybody always says, "It's the button on the top." Oh, thanks a lot. No shit, Sherlock, really, the button on the top right corner. Thanks for the heads-up, dipshit. Thanks for pointing that out, douchebag. I would have never figured it out. It's only been there since the dawn of time. Forever. Cavemen know how to take a photo. People, I don't think we need to say that anymore: "It's the button on the right corner of the camera." Just hand the fuckin' camera to somebody and say, "Can you please take a fuckin' photo? Thanks."

Reminds me of a funny story. A couple of months ago I'm closing up at the bar. I'm checking the floor for anything left behind when I notice this girl's handbag. It's hanging from one of the hooks under the bar. I look through it for ID so I can see who owns it. I can't see anything. No ID, nothing. So I dig in a little further and notice a bunch of photos in this case. I open the case up to see if I possibly know who owns the bag. Well, I certainly find out who owns the bag. I see pictures of a lady I know. Butt-arsed naked and getting shagged in more ways than I care to know about, and by more people than I care to remember. This lady was one hell of a swinger—a real porn star. Well, I leave the bag behind the bar with the anticipation of seeing her the next night. Sure enough, she shows up—the porn star—and asks me if I found a bag the night before. "Yes, indeed, I did," I tell her. "I found your bag alright." "How did you know it was my bag?" she asks. "I recognized you from the pictures, luv." "Good," she says. "I'm glad you liked them. I left them for you." Hello!

We're going out tomorrow night, Smithy. I'll send you the pictures.

Well, don't forget to tip your bartender, photos optional.

SEVENTEEN

Sunday, December 5, 2004
Is America Overweight?

I was reading an article in *The New York Times* today that said, "Obesity is at epidemic levels in America." So what they are saying is, "Laziness is at epidemic levels in America." Give me a break! They say, "Obesity is a disease"— no, it's not. Leprosy is a disease; diabetes is a disease; obesity is not a disease. They say it's a "glandular thing." No, it's a fuckin' greed thing. They say, "No, I'm just big-boned." Yes, that's right, big bones covered in meat and gravy. Stop eating fast food and walk once in a while, ya lazy fuckers. I'm lucky; I live in New York City where we walk all the time, and that certainly helps. Get off your arse, America.

I'm in the Cheyenne Diner reading this article, and I notice how greedy people can be. For instance, you get free coffee refills in most diners, but as I sit here I notice how much people can really abuse this. Would you have seven cheeseburgers if you got free refills? Actually, that's probably a bad example, because most Americans would. Stop drinking all the coffee, you greedy bastards. I was talking to this guy at the bar the other night, and he told me that he was in England and Ireland recently and was disappointed that when he ordered a sandwich in a deli, he only got two pieces of meat in it, whereas in America you get half a pig—about twenty slices of meat. I told him that in Ireland and England they make their sandwiches to fit their mouths.

I'm actually on a diet right now myself; it's that diet where you eat a lot of vegetables and drink lots of beer. I've lost ten pounds and my driver's license. I got invited to a vegetarian BBQ—that doesn't even make sense. Only in America.

There's another new diet out right now. It's called wear a black shirt!

Speaking of being overweight and fat, have you seen Magic Johnson recently? He's getting fatter and fatter. The only thing fatter with AIDS is . . .

Nigeria.

What we all need to do is start eating healthy and stay out of fast-food joints like McDonald's, Burger King, and Kentucky Fried Chicken. Burger King has a new breakfast sandwich called the Meat Lover's Breakfast. This consists of bacon, steak, sausage, more steak, and of course, eggs. That's supposed to be for one person. What the fuck? When you are unable to see your feet anymore, maybe it's time to stop eating this way. Kentucky Fried Chicken has also gotten involved. They have a chicken sandwich now where they have replaced the bread buns with pieces of chicken. So now you're just eating three pieces of chicken—holy shit. Personally, I think KFC is a bit like sex—it's great while you're doing it, but afterward you feel a wee bit dirty and your hands are sticky.

My advice to anyone who thinks they might be overweight: if you want to lose weight, don't eat anything that comes in a bucket—popcorn, Coca-Cola, ice cream, chicken, and so on. All come in a bucket. If it comes in a bucket, don't eat it. It's simple, right? Buckets belong on a farm, and if you keep eating from them, you will end up on one yourself.

By the way, did you ever notice that the people who are against abortion, you wouldn't want to fuck anyway? Thanks, George.

I see girls come into the bar all the time wearing tank tops. Listen, girls, if you're built like a tank, please don't wear the top.

Krispy Kreme donuts are now coming out with drinkable donuts—good news for fat people who don't want to chew. I rest my case.

I read in a magazine (did a lot of reading today, Smithy) that by the time I was finished reading the article, twenty people will have died from hunger. My question is: how do they know how quickly I read the article? If I just skim the article, will only ten people have died? I had to read it again. I think I just killed forty people.

The people over here are mad. For one thing they are either fat as a house or fitness crazy. All running around like headless chickens, drinking their power shakes. You know what the hardest thing is about rollerblading? Telling your parents you're gay. That's for all those rollerblade fuckheads who fly around all over the place and continually get in my way. The women are dead sexy!

Ever see these speed walkers with their legs and arms flying around? It's like they're having a heart attack or something. I met one the other day and I said to him, "What the fuck are you doing?" He said, "I'm exercising and losing weight." I said, "You're losing friends; you look ridiculous. Stop it."

Talking about exercising and all that, are there rules that the older you are at the gym, the more naked you need to be? Just a thought.

I go up to this guy at the gym who has muscles on top of muscles. I say to him, "Okay, pal, you win."

So please, America, get healthy. We can do it. I need your tips!

EIGHTEEN

Wednesday, December 22, 2004
Drugs

More and more these days, I notice women putting napkins on top of their drinks before they go outside to smoke. This is apparently supposed to prevent people from putting roofies—the date rape drug—in their drinks. Do you really think a napkin will prevent this from happening? Oh my God, she put a flimsy napkin on top of her drink? How will I ever put a roofie in there now? I'd better try another drink, preferably one that doesn't have a *heavy* napkin on top of it. It has really made it so much harder for me!

By the way, Smithy, did you ever notice that the ugliest girls in the bar are always the ones more concerned about getting a roofie? Sorry, luv, but there are at least six or seven women ahead of you.

Funny story, Smithy! Remember the car I bought a few years ago? Well, I decided to head to Upstate New York with a girlfriend for the weekend. We figured we would leave after I finished work Friday night to get a head start and beat the traffic. I finish up about four thirty and we head away. We are crossing over the George Washington Bridge when I notice a car pulled over on the side of the bridge with its emergency lights flashing. There's hardly any traffic, so I pull up behind them. The driver gets out and explains that he thinks he ran out of gas. I tell him there's a gas station just on the other side of the bridge. "Get in your car and I will push your car to the gas station." Off we go, and in no time we are pulling into the station. There's a slight hill down as we enter the station, so he just rolls right in. I get out and check to make sure he's all right. "Oh, thanks so much. Let me give you something; you really saved me, you have no idea," he says. He starts to reach into a large, black bag in the back of his car. "Don't worry about it, man. Glad you're okay." I head back to my car, reverse a bit, pull up beside him as his car is getting gassed up, and say, "Good luck." As we pull away, he throws a small bag into the car.

"Thanks, enjoy," he says. We're a bit startled, but we continue on anyway. As we continue north on the Palisades Parkway, my girlfriend reaches down to see what he tossed into the car. It's something wrapped up in black tape. "Should I open it?" she says. "Fuck it, why not?" As she pulls at the tape on one side, white powder starts to come out. "I think it's cocaine."

So this lad whom we helped out flings a bag of cocaine into our car. Unbelievable, right, Smithy? He must have had a shitload of it in his car if he was willing to give away the amount that he gave us. Had a hell of a weekend!

There's this guy Tommy who comes into the bar from time to time, maybe once a week. He's well over three hundred pounds—that's over twenty-two stone, Smithy. Either way he's a fat fucker—more chins than a Chinese phonebook. Wherever he is sitting he's sitting beside you. He was sitting in the bar and the restaurant—at the same time. He had a threesome last night and he was all by himself. He had gastric bypass surgery last year and beat it. You get the message, Smithy. He's fat. Probably eats out of a bucket.

Well, he has a big coke problem—it's pretty clear to see. The old devil's dandruff. What I don't understand is, how can you be fat and have a coke problem? What is he snorting—sugar? I heard that he did so much cocaine that he got a personal handwritten thank-you letter from Pablo Escobar.

I have to admit it, I tried coke once, but I got the bottle stuck up my nose! I don't like coke; I just like the smell of it.

By the way, rectal drugs would be handy; you could hide them and take them at the same time—just a thought.

You know, Smithy—God knows, you know—I've got nothing against a little bit of weed and a wee bump of Charlie once in a while. I just think it's a gateway drug to more serious shite, like holidays to Mexico and going to see Pink Floyd tribute bands.

I have another customer who comes into the bar and is always fucked up on cocaine. The thing about New York is, you can get drugs very easily. It's not so much on a street corner anymore (which I would not recommend), but you can call up a delivery service and have it delivered in no time—it's very convenient. Thirty minutes or less, a lot like Domino's. It's amazing, the amount of people who do drugs in this town, and it's certainly not the druggies on the streets. From sixty-year-old businessmen to eighteen-year-old teenagers.

Anyway, it's only a matter of time before something bad happens to this guy. *Please not on my shift*, I always say to myself when I see him coming in. *Please don't die on my shift.* I don't want this guy dying on my shift and having to explain to the cops about all the drugs and so on. I have said to him before to cut out the drugs, but he obviously doesn't give a shite about himself or, more importantly, me. Obviously he can do whatever he wants on his own time, in his own house. I don't know this guy enough to really give a shite about him, but please don't die on my shift.

Then the best of them all is Charlie—that's what I nicknamed her. She's cut more lines than a crippled kid in Disney World. She's a lovely, very generous lady but always off her head. I saw her doing cocaine (Charlie) off the bathroom counter one night in the handicapped bathroom. (Maybe it was a Disney World thing.) I told her that she had to stop doing it in the bar. Whatever you want to do in your own personal life is your business, but you can't be doing it in the bar anymore. It's a business after all, and it's also illegal. I don't want to sound like a hypocrite—God knows I'm no angel, and I've certainly enjoyed the odd illegal narcotic and a wee bump here and there—but I don't go into your work and do illegal shite. I do it in the comfort of my own home—usually anyway!

So what she started to do was hide her drugs in the roof of the women's toilet at the Skylight Diner on the corner, popping in and out all night. You gotta appreciate her ingenuity.

By the way, all these stories are certainly not about pointing fingers, but more importantly, about sharing funny moments. I hope so anyway! If you can't laugh, what's the point? That's the true spirit that keeps us all going—a funny moment. Laughter has worked forever.

Did you know that Osama Bin Laden at one time wanted to poison all the cocaine and heroin that came from Afghanistan to America (as almost all the world's heroin comes from there)? So let me see, Smithy, let's stop and think about this for a minute. Bin Laden wanted to kill all the coke and heroin addicts in America. Oh, how would we ever get over the killing of all the drug addicts in America? How would we ever get over the loss of all them wonderful, stand-up citizens?

My friend Jim the janitor who works in the *Daily News* building on Thirty-Third Street just got fired for failing a drug test. Drug tests are good and should be done, I think, but do we have to drug test a janitor? What's the worst thing he's going to do—drop his mop? Listen, if you're forty years of age and you're a janitor, I think you should be able to smoke a joint.

I heard the worst pickup line last night at the bar: "You must work in a lumberyard because you've been giving me wood all night!"

This prick started banging on the bar to get my attention. Please don't bang on the bar if you want a drink. I don't go to McDonald's and bang on your counter when I want a Big Mac. What's the deal with McDonald's staff who pretend they don't understand you if you don't insert "Mc" before the item you are ordering? It has to be a McChicken sandwich; just a "chicken sandwich" gets blank looks. Well, I'll have a McStraw and jam it in your McEyes, ya fucking McTosser.

Talking about McTossers, Smithy, you ever notice all these coffee shops opening up all over the place? In New York City they're everywhere. There's one on every block, never mind Starbucks. Full of people who say "me too," "totally," or "really." Sitting for hours on their Apple computers, drinking lattes, pretending they are writing their number-one bestselling book. What a bunch of arseholes. You ever fantasize about running around just slapping all the cups of coffee and muffins out of their hands—or is that just me? Don't get me wrong, I love a nice cup of coffee, but you can't even get a cup of coffee anymore—a regular cup of "Joe." I went into a coffee shop last week and asked for a cup of coffee. The girl behind the counter said, "We have almond, hazelnut, mint, apple, banana," and so on. I said, "Could you please give me a regular cup of coffee for fuck's sake?" Well, she says, "We don't have regular; we have short, tall, grande, or venti." "Just give me a cup of tea then," I say. She says, "We have tazo, chai crème, vanilla, or green tea." I ask, "Do you have C.U.N.Tea?" Just kiddin'. She says, "No." I just go home and make myself a cup of tea. Sometimes you just gotta do it yourself, right, Smithy?

Restaurants are also trying to bullshit us with their fancy names for things like gourmet, hearty, or homestyle. The difference between food and all these fancy words is sixty dollars.

See ya soon, buddy. Sorry for the rant.

NINETEEN

Friday, December 31, 2004
Have You Seen My Gun?

It's New Year's Eve, New York City, 2004. It's jam-packed behind the bar. Everyone is having a great time. All is running smoothly. Not one arsehole in the crowd, which is amazing for this night. The cops start showing up after the Times Square ball drops—all is good. It's five deep at the bar in no time. Everyone is pretty much served—beers and whiskey shots, thank God. I'm in the weeds, as we say (when you don't even have time to put your head up), just listening to orders and grabbing money. Thank God no dickheads are ordering Alabama Slammers, martinis, or lemon drops.

Then I get the question, "Have you seen my gun?" Five words nobody ever wants to hear. "What?" I say, hoping I'm misunderstanding the question. "Have you seen my gun?" he repeats.

"No," I say. "I haven't seen your gun." Again, five words I never thought I would ever say.

As I finally look up to see who is asking me this question, it now makes total sense. It's my good friend Dutch, the cop. Remember him? Now I know he is telling the truth, as it's not the first time we have had "issues" with his gun. In the few years that I have known Dutch, we have put multiple holes in the ceiling of the bar. I have fired his gun out the window of his unmarked police car (really pissing off the highway cops), and it has been left in my apartment multiple times after many impromptu parties. It seems he really wants to get rid of it.

"Well, I suppose we better look for it, right?" I say to Dutch. So I get the torch out, don't announce to the bar what we are looking for—for obvious reasons—and as secretly as we can, we begin the search for the elusive gun. I'm shining the light between the many legs and underneath tables and chairs. All we find are pieces of glass, some dirty napkins, empty bottles, and a couple of indescribable items—the usual bar stuff. I would not be surprised if I found a few guns, handcuffs, and nightsticks in this bar. Well, not tonight; no luck so far. Most people are too drunk to even notice what we are doing.

So far, nothing at the bar or restaurant area. Then the bathrooms, again no sign. I say to Dutch, "Keep looking, I need to go back behind the bar for a few minutes." I'm thinking to myself, *If this lost gun gets into the wrong hands, who knows what could happen.* Remember, we're on the West Side of Manhattan—Hell's Kitchen. There are a lot of dodgy characters banging around these streets. I always have the odd gangster hanging around the bar.

Next, I go into the bathroom again, head into the last stall to go to the toilet, and lo and behold, what do I find? It's a gun. Holy shit, I think we've found it: a silver, shiny, nine gauge Smith & Wesson. Right in the middle of the bowl—a 9mm. Working in this bar, you become very knowledgeable of the many types of guns. Well, I hope it is a gun or else somebody has some serious digestive problems! I take my pen from behind my ear, and like a CSI detective, scoop it out of the toilet. I flag down the owner of the "Turd Gun" and "we" come up with the idea of putting it in the safe until the morning. Dutch says, "Sounds good. If not, just bring it home; I'll get it off you later. Give me a beer, will you? Thanks."

Well, Happy New Year, Smithy, and don't forget your guns and to tip your bartender.

Saturday, January 22, 2005
That's Drunks for Ya!

This drunken man walks into the bar yesterday with a key in his hand, stumbling back and forth. I'm obviously not going to serve him. So I say to him, "Can I help you, sir?" "Yessh! Ssssomebody sstole my carrr," the man replies. I ask, "Where was your car the last time you saw it?" "It wasss on the end of thisshh key," the man replies. I'm thinking to myself, *Thank God your car is gone.* About that time I look down and see the man's dick hanging out of his fly for the entire world to see. I ask the man, "Are you aware that you are exposing yourself?"

Momentarily confused, the drunk looks down at his crotch and without missing a beat, blurts out to me, "Holy shit, my girlfriend's gone too!"

You can't make this shit up. Have a great day, Smithy, and please don't forget to tip your bartenders!

Friday, February 18, 2005
Pepsi, My Favorite Brasser! (Hooker)

Remember Pepsi, Smithy, the local hooker who comes into the bar from time to time? I'm not sure if that's her real name, but she came into the bar last night. A very nice lady who happens to be a prostitute. In the Hell's Kitchen part of NYC, you still get your hookers here and there. It's not like the old days when they were everywhere. Thanks to Mayor Rudolf Giuliani, who was the mayor in the nineties in NYC; he really cleaned up the city. Ya, thanks a lot, Rudy. When she arrives, she always leaves me ten dollars and goes into the bathroom to wash up. She never stops. It's wash up and go out and make more money. Last night she comes in with a friend. I forget her friend's name; maybe it's Coke or Diet Pepsi as she was pretty skinny. Well, they decide to stop and have a drink, and because Pepsi has been very respectful over the years, I welcome the two ladies to the bar. I make them up two very dirty Grey Goose martinis with olives. Very expensive tastes. I would love to know what they charge. Maybe they just want to get the taste out of their mouths—who knows? After a while they start talking about blowjobs and how good they both think they are at them. They say to me, "Can you help us out here? We are trying to figure out who gives the best blowjob? Can we try out on you?" Well, always one to help out the ladies and to do it in the name of science, off we go. To make a long story short, pun intended, it was too close to call. I will take a tip like that anytime. I assume, Smithy, after me telling you the last story, you are on your way out to the airport.

That actually reminds me of another story, Smithy. This young lad comes into the bar and asks me for a beer and a shot. "Big night tonight?" I ask him. "Are you celebrating?" "Yes," he says. "I just had my first blowjob tonight." I say, "The drinks are on the house—congratulations, and best of luck to ya, man." Then he says, "Thanks a lot, these drinks should help get the taste out of my mouth."

You just never know, Smithy, do ya? Take care and talk to you soon.

Tuesday, March 15, 2005
It's Cold in the City Tonight

It's so cold tonight in New York City that the hookers in Times Square are blowing on soup. It's so cold I see one guy rubbing the Olsen twins together to start a fire. Colder than a witch's tit, or as we like to say, colder than a witch's Walter Mitties. It's a few degrees short of fuckin' freezing.

On cold nights like these, I always try to go and look for my homeless friend, Richie. He lives on West Thirty-Sixth Street in the back of a parking lot behind two dumpsters, in a box. I usually bring him some food that is left over from our kitchen or a coat that has been in the lost-and-found box too long. I microwaved it (the food, that is), but by the time I get there it's pretty cold, but it's food, right? I get to Thirty-Sixth Street and I shout into the back of the lot for Richie. "You around, Richie? You there?" He always comes out smiling. He always has a good outlook on things—really puts things into perspective. Richie comes into the bar from time to time, usually late in the evening with a handful of coins that he has collected throughout the night. He maybe has a couple of dimes and a few quarters and says, "Can I have ten dollars for this?" He's usually at least five dollars short—smart little fucker—but I like him. He tells me that he would rather be on the street. As he says, "No worries or bills on the street." But on nights like these, I don't think so. Let's hope Richie makes it, even if it's just tonight.

As I always say, "Don't forget to tip your bartender," but on cold nights like these where the difference between life and death could be a few dollars to a homeless guy, please give them to Richie. Peace.

I was on the subway the other day with a big bag of change, on my way to the coin machine at Commerce Bank on Forty-Second Street and Ninth Avenue, when I realized it was not a good idea. What's the last thing you want to see on the way to cash in change at the local bank? That's right: homeless people. Because of the cold weather right now, all the homeless people are in the subways trying to keep warm. Everywhere I went I heard the same thing: "Any spare change?" And me with a big bag of spare change. When I finally got to the bank I had no spare change—fuckin' homeless.

By the way, I've never seen a homeless fella with a bottle of Gatorade. Have you, Smithy?

Quick story: Abdul and Paddy are beggars outside Port Authority Bus Station on Forty-Second Street. Abdul has a Mercedes, a large house in the suburbs, and loads of money. Paddy has fuck all. Abdul's begging hat is always overflowing with money; Paddy's usually only has a few coins in it. "How do you do it?" asks Paddy. "Look at your sign," says Abdul. Paddy reads his sign: "Out of work and wife and six kids need support." Then he reads Abdul's: "I only need another ten dollars to get back to Afghanistan."

I don't like American women; I like Al Qaeda women because they're the "bomb."

A homeless man asked me, "Can I have three hundred dollars for a cup of coffee?" I told him, "Coffee's a dollar," and he said, "Yeah, but I want to drink it in Brazil."

Another one came up to me saying, "I haven't eaten in two days." I said, "You should really force yourself." That was for the other smart fucker.

The homeless can be very funny and imaginative, and when they are, you have to give it up, I think. Richie comes into the bar late at night and helps me out if I need anything. He usually hangs out around the entrance to the Lincoln Tunnel with a big sign saying, LET'S DO LUNCH—YOU PAY. Pretty funny, right?

He says this all the time, and I also hear this from people at the bar: "Live every day like it's your last." I'm all for that idea. I even tried it one day; however, I wouldn't recommend it.

One Tuesday a few weeks ago, I woke up, quit my job, shagged my girlfriend's sister, and kicked a cop in the arse. Wednesday rolled around and to my surprise and great disappointment, I had no job, no girlfriend, and was in jail. One good thing: I got a new girlfriend named Bubba.

I couldn't go to jail. Do you know what happens to skinny lads like me in jail, Smithy? That's right—they usually hang themselves after their first shower. Plus I don't like the taste of prison food or penis.

My mate went to jail recently. His first month in jail he had his appendix out. The second month he had his tonsils and gall bladder removed. The prison warden thinks he's trying to escape . . . bit by bit!

Cheers, Smithy.

TWENTY

Wednesday, April 13, 2005
Freud You!

Pretty quiet night tonight. These two people walk into the bar tonight—not a couple, as they are a little bit awkward toward each other, but they are obviously friends. So I say, "Hi, what are you having?" The guy says right away, "I'll have a bottle of Bud." The girl takes her time, can't make up her mind . . . obviously first time in a bar! Right away I know this person: pain in the arse, crying out for attention, never got a hug as a child, wants the world to wait on her. However, these people can be interesting and sometimes fun! Eventually she asks for a rum and Coke—after all that. So about ten minutes pass and she says, "Do you know how to make a cosmopolitan?" (Vodka, triple sec, lime juice, and cranberry juice.) "Yes," I say, and her friend orders another Bud. Another ten to twenty minutes pass, and then she says to me, "Can you make me a Black Russian? Do you know how to make it?" I say, "Listen, you know, luv, this is not my first night." "Oh, really," she says. "Looks like it is."

So this is where the fun begins, Smithy. She finishes the earlier cosmopolitan, and while I'm in the middle of a conversation with another customer, she shouts, "Take my empty glass away. Do you know how to be a bartender?" Then she starts calling me all sorts of names, none of which are especially original.

I look at her, laugh, and continue my conversation. You need to nip that in the bud right away or else they will walk all over you. Listen, I know my job detail, but I'm a human being behind this bar, as well. There's not oil running through my veins.

Then she says, "What's wrong with you? Where are you from? What month were you born? Why do you hate yourself?" and so forth. I say, pretending to cry, "Maybe I just need a hug." I then say, just to keep it fun, "Darling, enough of the psychobabble bullshit. Save it for someone who cares. You know what

Freud said? The Irish are impervious to psychoanalyses. Let it go, sweetheart." "Don't you think I'm a beautiful woman? Do you not want me?" she says. "Beauty comes in many forms," I say, "but you are so ugly on the inside. Are you afraid of the Big Bad Wolf?" I ask. "No," she says. "That's funny," I say to her, "as the other two pigs were."

So now she does a total 360 on me—she tells me that she lives up the street and wants me to shag her. Typical girl who looks confident on the outside: mean and aggressive, goes through her whole life hating and being mean to people, when in reality she hates herself and is so insecure. I say to her, "You have the sex appeal of a school bus fire. I wouldn't fuck you with his cock"— pointing at her friend. Before you get upset with me, Smithy, trust me, she had it coming, and now maybe she will not be such a bitch to people in the future. Eventually her friend says to her, "You're being an asshole, time to go home." Best of luck to you, darling. You're going to need it.

Remember, Smithy, we're not just bartenders—we are psychiatrists too.

Friday, April 15, 2005
Full Moon Tonight

It was one of those nights that every bartender knows and feels before they happen. It started out when I came into work at 6 p.m. to start my night. There is this drunk at the end of the bar, and right away I'm pissed off that he is still in the bar and being served. It doesn't take much to piss off the start of the night for a night bartender; we are very fragile, you know. So the day bartender says to me, "Don't serve that guy, he's fucked up," but it was okay for you to serve him, and why would you care, you're out of here anyway— fucking prick. So I say, "You served him—you get rid of him." "I didn't serve him," he says. I say, "Where did he get the Heineken? Listen, why don't you think before you talk; I'm sick of you serving obviously fucked-up people and saying, 'You have a good night,' and then running out the door, only for me to handle the shit you leave behind." If you're a night bartender you know what I'm talking about. Well, I eventually get this fuckhead out of the bar after he comes in a few more times not realizing that I just kicked him out before. Unfortunately my night goes from bad to worse.

A few hours go by, and all of a sudden a major brawl starts up. It's not a handbag and pocketbook fight or a shoving match; these people really wanted to hurt each other. Broken bottle, chairs, tables, and blood everywhere—an extremely volatile atmosphere.

These fights happen at best once a year. What I have learned over the years as a bartender is not to be a hero. I have loved ones to go home to. Fights usually break themselves up. Don't be a hero. They bury heroes. As the Marines and the Rangers say, "We don't die for our country—we live for our country." If anybody knows me, I'm not the one to run from a fight, but this shite is ridiculous. They don't pay me enough. Mind you, there are some nights in the bar when I'm like, fuck, I would love a bit of action right now. A good beating, a bit of anarchy, get in close to somebody and really give it a go. Remember, I have an advantage: I'm sober . . . well, usually anyway. Listen, if a fight lasts more than ten seconds and you're in it, you're in big trouble. So remember that when a fight starts and you're working behind a bar, by the time you get around the bar the fight is usually over, but if the fight is still going on after you get around the bar, that's a fight you have no business getting in, and you certainly do not want to be in it. So stay behind the bar and clear all the money off it. The fight eventually spilled out onto the street—somebody else's problem now.

So here's to the full moon tonight, Smithy, and a full tip jar.

TWENTY-ONE

Tuesday, April 19, 2005
Pope Benedict—Holy Shite!

We have a new pope. What do you think, Smithy? What does Ireland think about the new pope? Catholic Ireland. I know the last time we had a German in power, and a balcony, we had no problems, right? Ah, for fuck's sake, let's hope history doesn't repeat itself. Hail, Benedict. I suppose we will give him the Benedict of the doubt!

You know I can tell that joke, Smithy. My grandfather had to hide from the Nazis during the war, in Ireland, his whole life, and he was not even Jewish. Pope Benedict—he's the 265th gay pope!

Did you know, Smithy, that we were actually supposed to get a different pope? His name was Sacola, but the Church felt that his name did not sound right. You know, "Pope Sacola." (Think about it—I'll give ya a second.)

The new pope is believed to have gotten the bird flu. They think he might have gotten it from one of the cardinals. Now we have the swine flu. However, there is something even more serious than that: the turtle flu. It's coming slowly, but it's coming. Just wait and see.

There was this priest in the bar last night—from Saint Catherine's Church around the corner on Thirty-Fourth Street. I will not say his name, but he was a bit of a prick, to be honest. Actually, I recently went to see him, as I was asked by my friends Nick and Mona to be the godfather of their baby. The priest wanted to meet the godfather for the upcoming christening. Well, to make a long story painful, when I went to see him, he made me feel about as welcome as a fart in a spaceman's suit. He asked me if I was registered to his church. I didn't know what he meant, so I said "no."

Did you know that you now have to register to go to mass? It's turning into the Department of Motor Vehicles, for fuck's sake. By the way, and at the risk of oversharing, did you know that black people invented the Department of

Motor Vehicles? Ya, it was to get white people back for slavery—fair enough, I think!

Well, anyway, this is what this messenger of Christ said to me. (Who knew? I wonder, will it involve a donation?) He basically wanted to know if I was a Catholic. I tell him I am and that I actually go to his church once in a while. He says, "I've never seen you here before," and starts quizzing me on what times do the masses start and so forth. I didn't realize there was going be a test or I would have studied.

Well, he says, "I suppose I will have to believe you." I'm thinking to myself, *Why don't you shove your church up your arse*? Now, I'm not a practicing Catholic (I have it down good now), but I do know right from wrong, and this big bollox is out of line. I keep my comments to myself, as I just want my friends' christening to go well. Don't want to let me ma down, you know. She raised me right. Again he asks me if I can register with the church. I give him twenty dollars and leave. I'm now officially registered and a Catholic again!

Here's where it gets interesting. The same priest comes into the bar last night and asks me for a glass of wine. I give him a glass of water and tell him to "make it himself." Now before you get upset with me, he did make me feel earlier about as welcome as a black man at a KKK meeting. We're really busy at the bar and there are no tables available for dinner. I can see the priest is getting a wee bit annoyed at the wait. I say to him, "You will get the next table." Well, every two minutes, he keeps asking me, "Is the table ready? Is the table ready?" Like a kid asking his parents if they are there yet. So I say to him, "Listen, Father, if you'd like, you can register for a table." With that, he storms out, all pissed off. I thought at least one of the things you need as a priest is patience and a sense of humor! Unfortunately Father Cranky had neither.

The Catholic Church is cock-tickling their way into bankruptcy. You can't really blame the priests however, because a lot of them started out as altar boys and just got sucked into it.

By the way, Christians must be sick in the head. Only someone who hates himself could possibly think of the pleasures of masturbation as self-abuse.

I met this priest a couple of weeks ago at the bar, Smithy. I asked him why he wears his collar back to front. He said, "Because I'm a father." I said, "My dad is a father and he doesn't wear his collar back to front." The priest said, "Oh, no, you don't understand—I'm the father of millions." I told him, "I think it's your trousers you should be wearing back to front."

Religion is all about recognition, you know. The Jews don't recognize the Palestinians as the settlers of Jerusalem. The Protestants don't recognize the pope as the leader of the Christians, and the Mormons don't recognize each other in Hooters.

That reminds me, these two priests were having dinner together at the bar. I didn't know whether or not to send them over a bottle of wine or a Cub Scout! What do you call a gay priest? A priest. I think I'm going to hell for that one.

While I'm going to hell—a priest, a rapist, and a pedophile walk into a bar . . . and that was just the first guy!

See ya in hell, Smithy, and remember to tip your bartender!

Monday, May 2, 2005
McHale's Pub

So, Smithy, I'm in McHale's today—one of my favorite bars in Midtown, on Eight Avenue and Forty-Sixth Street—having some lunch with a few mates. I'm walking through the dark, red-lit back room to go to the bathroom when I notice Bono and The Edge in the corner of the restaurant. I walk over to them and say, "Jaysus, lads, things must be rough if the both of ya are splitting a hamburger?" They laugh and ask me where I'm from, to which I say, "Dublin." Bono, in his best northside Dublin accent says, "Ah, fair play to ya."

McHale's is a legendary NYC bar—one of the great old school watering holes in Midtown—and is known for many things: a stagehand's bar, a place to leave your Broadway tickets for pickup (tip the bartender), a hockey bar, and for having the best and biggest burgers in the city (literally the size of the plate). The storied bar also appeared in the classic NYC film *Sleepers*, as well as *Money Train* and *She's the One*. I sit down beside them and tell them what a big fan I am. I go on to recall the numerous times I saw them in concert—I'm sure to the delight of them both. I tell them I would love to buy them a drink. I order three shots of whiskey, and we knock them back. I bleedin' pay for them too!

All joking aside, they were cool, and I'm sure they get sick of fuckers like me annoying them. About an hour passes and they give me a wave as they sneak out the side door onto Forty-Sixth Street and into an awaiting black SUV. I'm there with my two friends, and they start slagging me, saying, "You and Bono meeting up later to save the world?" "Fuck off; you're just jealous," I say. We go to pay the bill, when the bartender says, "Bono and The Edge picked up your check." Nice one, lads.

TWENTY-TWO

Wednesday, May 18, 2005
A Shot in the Dark?

S mithy, I wake up this morning to the sound of my home phone. I don't answer it because it's only eight o'clock in the morning and I had just rolled into bed a few hours earlier. And the only calls we generally get at home are some fuckers selling insurance or begging for something. My roommate's an awful cunt for not paying his bills. He got a call last week about not paying his student loan back. The man on the phone informed him that they hadn't received his last loan payment. He informed them that they had.

Anyway, the phone goes to voicemail and it's the owner of the pub. You'd know his thick country accent anywhere. "What the fuck happened last night? Give me a call right away," the message goes. *Ah, fuck, what did I do last night?* I'm doing the checklist in my head: did the cash, locked it up in the safe, turned off all the lights, set the alarm. What could he be calling about? Oh, wait a minute. I wonder if it has anything to do with the shooting in the ceiling of the bar?

Yup, Smithy, it had to do with the shooting in the ceiling. Here's what happened: We were fooling around last night, and a bunch of us started shooting this cop's gun into the ceiling of the bar. We do it from time to time, as you know. It can get pretty wild late at night sometimes. I call him back and he says, "What was going on last night?" "Nothing," I say. "What?" he says a little louder. "I found six fresh bullet holes in the ceiling and some shells on the floor. Then the man from the office upstairs came down."

Apparently for some strange reason the bullets we fired went through the old tin ceiling and then through the desk of the man who has an office upstairs. They never do that!

So he comes into his office to find six holes in his new mahogany desk. Six new pen holders. Upon further review he notices matching holes underneath his desk coming from the floorboards. He can see clear through to the bar. He comes marching down to the bar in the morning and says, I quote, "This shit needs to stop. If this happens again I'm going to the cops." Little did he know it was them in the first place!

Fuck, I think to myself, trying to remember quickly what exactly happened so I can tell him something. I say, "Oh ya, there were a few old-timers in last night and they shot a few holes in the ceiling. Just blowing off some steam after work." "Who was it?" he asks. "Was it Dutch?" He knows Dutch the cop is a good pal of mine. Remember, Smithy, Dutch who lost his gun New Year's Eve? "No," I say, lying through my teeth. I know who they were, but I'm not going to tell him—considering three of the holes belong to me. I say, "You know what, I can't remember their names. I don't see them too often." (Even though they're my good buddies from Midtown South Police Station.) "What did they look like?" he asks. I describe a mix of four or five different people so as not to really describe anyone in particular—to try and confuse him. He mentions a few names, and he's bang-on, by the way—except for me. I say, "No, that's not them." "Tell them cops to stop fucking around and firing their guns," he says. "One of these days somebody will get hurt." You know what, Smithy, he's right, but for fuck's sake, it's such a rush firing a gun!

So tonight I'm telling the cops what happened earlier, and just as I'm finishing they pop two more in the roof, this time in a different location. "Better not hit his desk again," they say.

Crazy fuckers.

The reason Midtown South cops come into the bar is because technically my bar is not in their precinct. The city frowns upon cops hanging out in bars in their own precinct. So because we are on the west side of Ninth Avenue, they're technically not in their own precinct. It's a difference of about twenty feet. When you come over, I will show you the bullet holes. Put some in yourself if you want—make your own mark. As I said before, it's like Swiss cheese.

Sunday, May 29, 2005
My Aunt Died

Well, today, Smithy, my favorite Irish aunt died. You remember her. She certainly lived a great, long life. She was actually 106 years young when she died, so don't feel too bad. We used to call her "antique." She used to go up to statues and say to people, "I fucked him." She used to go into the store Old Navy looking for sailors.

Today my friend Dave actually asked me how she died. Oh, she died of a heart attack after teaching a crunch yoga class; she died of a heart attack in the mosh pit at a Metallica concert; her chute didn't open . . . . She was 106, everybody! By the way, what's the difference between an Irish wedding and an Irish funeral? One less drunk. Rest in peace!

Cheers to my aunt! Now go out and have a drink, and tip your bartender!

Friday, June 10, 2005
Lawyers

I have a lawyer friend who comes into the bar from time to time. He's a nice guy, but he's a lawyer, so you have to fuck with them.

I said to him, "What's the difference between a prostitute and a lawyer? A prostitute will stop fucking you when you're dead. How do you know when a lawyer is lying? When he opens his mouth."

A guy comes into the bar shouting and screaming the other night saying, "All lawyers are arseholes, all lawyers are arseholes, all lawyers are arseholes." This man runs up to him and says, "I'm offended by that." The other guy says, "What, are you a lawyer?" "No," he says. "I'm an arsehole."

What is black and brown and looks good around a lawyer's neck? A Doberman.

He's not the brightest lawyer in the world; he thought an affidavit was a Jewish wine.

This woman goes to the doctor and asks, "Can women get pregnant from anal sex?" "Of course they can," says the doctor. "Where do you think lawyers come from?"

So he says to me, "Why are there no Irish lawyers? Because they can't pass the bar."

I suppose I had that one coming. Cheers!

Wednesday, June 29, 2005
Artie the Jew!

My good old Jewish friend Artie comes into the bar tonight, all happy and smiling. Right there I know something's wrong. When was the last time you saw a Jew smile? I ask him, "Why are you so happy, Artie?" Doing the Jewish sign of the cross—spectacles, testicles, wallet, and watch—he tells me he just won the New York State Lottery—ten million dollars, to be exact. Drinks for everybody. Well, after the bar slows down, I ask him, "So, Artie, what's next? What are you going to do with your winnings?" Now, let me tell you a little about Artie, Smithy. He's a tough fucker: eighty-nine years old, survived the Holocaust, was in a concentration camp during the war—basically he's seen and been through it all. He says, "First, I'm going to donate half of the winnings—that's five million dollars—to the Nazi party." I'm like, "What? Are you losing your mind?" "No," he says, "I'm going to donate half the winnings—that's five million—to the Nazi party."

I say, "Why would you do that after what they did to you and your people?" "Well, it's like this," he says, while rolling up his sleeves—"THEY GAVE ME THE NUMBERS!"

There is a God after all, Smithy.

My friend Artie has a great sense of humor. Here's another story he told me recently that I thought you might enjoy, Smithy:

A Jewish entrepreneur has a spoiled son and decides the only way to teach his son responsibility is to teach him the family business.

He pulls him out of the University of Miami and puts him to work in the family nail business. After a few days, the kid has his first idea to help the business.

He says, "Dad, when I was coming home from college I saw a giant billboard outside the Lincoln Tunnel while I was going into New York City. We should buy an ad there since I saw lots of construction trucks in the tunnel, and they're our customers." The father says, "Go set this up with our advertising director. Don't bother me with the details; I'm going on vacation to Boca, Florida"—like all Jewish businessmen do.

The father is coming home from Boca, and as he approaches the Lincoln Tunnel he sees the billboard. It has a picture of Christ being crucified on the cross, and the words underneath read, THE ROMANS USED SCHWARTZ'S NAILS.

He goes nuts, calls his son on his cell phone, and screams, "You good-for-nothing spoiled brat, cocaine addict idiot! Most of our customers are Christian! I'm so upset, I'm going back to Boca, and you better get this straightened out or I'm gonna cut your balls off!"

The old man goes back to Boca for two weeks, and the next time he comes through the Lincoln Tunnel he sees the billboard. It has a picture of Christ lying on the ground. Underneath it, it reads, THIS IS WHAT HAPPENS WHEN YOU DON'T USE SCHWARTZ'S NAILS.

This reminds me, these three lads were talking at the bar. The first one says, "Isn't it funny how people get nicknames—how nicknames start? For instance, people call me Shorty, and I'm six foot five." The next lad says, "That's true, I don't have a hair on my head, and they call me Curly." The last lad pipes in and says " Yes, lads, it's so true. They call me the fuckin' Jew, and I haven't got laid in years."

It's only a joke. That one's for Artie. Mind you, this is the same guy who thought Irving Berlin was a Jewish section of Germany.

By the way, don't fuck with the Jews. They cut the tops off their own penises. Imagine what they will do to yours . . . .

Well, Smithy, I told you he has a good sense of humor. Good luck, and hope to see you soon—and please don't forget to tip your bartender!

TWENTY-THREE

Tuesday, April 4, 2006
The "Westies"

This guy in the bar tonight threatens to shoot me. It's always the same; the loudest person in the bar is usually the weakest. You should watch the quiet guy in the corner; he's the one who you need to worry about. People who tell you they are in the Mob or the Westies and are going to kill you—they usually aren't and don't. By the way, the Westies were an Irish gang that "controlled," but more like "terrorized" the Hell's Kitchen part of New York City, mostly during the seventies and eighties. There's a great book called *The Westies* written by T.J. English that you should read. The TV likes to glorify these people, but believe me, it's like the ones in Ireland, Smithy—there's nothing admirable about them. They think they're heroes. They're not. A hero is somebody who gets up every morning and goes to work. These wankers have never done an honest day's work in their lives.

I obviously don't know them all, but the ones I've met (except for a few) have been nothing but wankers. I've met a few who were fair, old school gangsters who had respect for people and the neighborhood. I have actually become good friends with one lad. He did time for stabbing a fellow gang member in the eye during a fight in Dave's Tavern on Ninth Avenue. He did his time and now just wants to move on peacefully with his life. There's nothing more American than a second chance.

Don't get me wrong, I love a good caper and a wee hustle here and there, but not at the expense of innocent, working-class people. Scam all the banks and insurance companies that you want.

Anyway, they come in all sneaky, under the banner of "I'm just trying to protect the neighborhood and keep it safe." Like they're your pals, but in reality they are just selfish cunts who are only interested in what's best for them. I had this clown come in one night and "recommend" that we should buy whiskey from him, at twice what we were paying.

Oh ya, we're here to protect the neighborhood.

Unfortunately, once in a while some of the scumbags from the Westies surface from the sewers of NYC. The fact that my bar is in Hell's Kitchen only adds to the frequency of their visits.

As I said earlier, it all started when this prick walked into the bar tonight and asked for a Heineken and a chilled shot of Patron tequila. Right away I don't like this person, and my gut tells me he's no good. Your gut usually never lets you down. I give him the drinks, but no "thank you" or "please" to be had. Then he says, "Put the college basketball game on." Just like that, again no "please" or "thank you"—just "put the college basketball game on." I tell him, "Somebody is watching the Knicks basketball game already on that TV, so I can't change the channel." I didn't want to change the channel anyway for this rude prick.

So with that he says to me, "Put the fucking game on." Now I say, "Listen, you fuckin' wanker, that TV is never going to be changed now, so get the fuck out of here. Did your mother ever tell you never to drink on an empty head?"

Here's where the fun starts: "Do you not know who you're dealing with?" he says. "I'm connected." I say, "Yes, that's right; you're connected alright—to a fuckin' arsehole." "I'm in the Westies, and you're a dead man," he says. "I'm going to fucking shoot you." Again he says, "Put the fucking game on." Again I say, "Listen, scumbag, first of all you're about twenty years too late, and second, hell will freeze over before I change that TV channel, so get the fuck out of here. You're a fuckin' nobody, just like me." Eventually he leaves after threatening me a few more times. Now he starts calling up the bar, saying he is going to shoot me and that he is waiting outside the door with a gun. "Whatever," I say, "you fuckin' loser." He keeps calling and calling and then I notice his name and phone number showing up on the caller ID on the phone. A real Einstein, a real professional gangster. He keeps calling, saying, "Do you not know who I am?" I actually say, "Yes, I know who you are. Your name and number are coming up on the caller ID." "I'm in the Westies," he says again, "so fucking listen to what I say."

I say, "Did ya ever hear of the IRA? They would make the Westies look like a bunch of Girl Scouts—now fuck off and stop wasting my time."

Then he walks back into the bar and I say, "Fuck you, this ends right now." As he is entering the bar, I push him back out the door and into the garbage outside—a perfect place for this piece of shite. I walk back in the bar, and sure enough, the dickhead starts calling again. This time he has changed his tune; now he wants to sue me. He says, "You hurt me. I'm going to sue you and the bar." I say, "Make your mind up—are you going to kill me or sue me, because it's very hard to sue a dead man," and I hang up. Again a few minutes go by, and again he calls up, but this time I just laugh at him and I hand it to an off-duty police officer in the bar who had just come in. The cop says to this tough guy, "Listen, idiot, what you're doing right now is verbal harassment, punishable up to a year in jail. I have your name and number from the caller ID, and if you don't stop calling, I will personally go to your home and grab you out of your house by your balls, and you will pay. Also, if I ever see you around here again, I will kick your ass—got it?"

Now the tough guy starts bawling, crying, saying how sorry he is and how all he wanted was for the bartender to put the game on. What a scumbag loser.

Fortunately these things happen only once in a while—and we all need a good laugh now and again, don't we?

Wednesday, April 5, 2006
Tenth Anniversary of Larry LaPrise's Passing

With all the sadness and trauma going on around the world at the moment, it is worth reflecting on the death of a very important person. Ten years ago today, Larry LaPrise, the man who wrote the classic song "Hokey Pokey," died peacefully at home at the age of eighty-three. It's always been a very popular song at my bar. Anyway, the most traumatic part for his family was getting him in the coffin. They put his left leg in, and then the trouble started!

That reminds me of a good bar joke. As you know, a good bartender must always be ready to tell a joke. As I said before, my mother used to say to me when I was younger, "Never let the truth get in the way of a good story," so this one's for you, Mum.

There's this funeral parade going up this steep hill in Harlem, when all of a sudden the coffin slides out the back of the hearse and starts speeding down the hill. Everyone is chasing after it. It starts moving faster and faster, and nobody can catch it until it flies past the Apollo Theater on 125th Street and across the street and into a pharmacy. It crashes through the door of the pharmacy and stops right at the counter just as the body pops right up out of the coffin. The pharmacist behind the counter says, "Can I help you?" and the body says, "Can you give me something to stop my coughin'?"

Friday, May 19, 2006
Why Did You Call Me a "Cunt"?

This girl comes in late last night, and right off the bat I know she is trouble. She starts shouting orders at me, no "please" or "thank you" in sight. Maybe she's in the Westies as well. She spills her drink all over the bar and demands for me to clean it up right away. Then she demands that I make her a new drink at no charge. Again no "please" or "thank you" anywhere. I say, "I did not spill your drink. If you want another one, you will have to pay for it." I would have made her another drink, no charge, if she had only had some manners. She starts screaming obscenities at me, so I say, "Ah, you're a funny cunt, aren't ya?" World War III begins as she starts screaming. "Fuck you! Why did you call me a cunt? I have three degrees and make ten times what you make! Fuck you!" "Piss off, would ya?" I say.

She says, "I'm street smart, too." "Ya, Sesame Street smart," I say. Again she starts screaming, grabbing people at the bar. "Why did you call me a cunt? Why did you call me a cunt?" "Close your mouth before somebody considers it an invitation." (Maybe I went a wee bit too far with that one!)

Listen, people think that the word *cunt* is a bad word. Well, it's not; it's just a word. Women, you need to get over the word *cunt* and any other so-called bad words. The more you say it, the less offensive it becomes, and you take the poison out of it—come on. Like any word, if you say it in anger, that's when it might become offensive, but I was just taking the piss. It was America who ruined the word *cunt*. They think it is some kind of derogatory term for a vagina, or someone who has one, but it has never been that way in Ireland, where I hail from, or for that matter, the rest of the world.

Anyway, in Ireland and most of the world, the word *cunt* is happy and cheery, like *fuckin' brilliant* and *shite*, or *awesome* in America. You know, the word *cunt* comes from the Latin word *cuinty*, meaning barren place. So let it go, everyone. Where I come from, the word *cunt* is used so much that in many ways it is used to compliment someone. For example, she's a funny cunt, I like that cunt, and he's a cool cunt. So again, let it go—only then will it become just four letters. Go rent a Lenny Bruce CD or DVD; he was the master of comedy and a real funny cunt!

By the way, the Aussies have really mastered the word. They say it so well, with precise timing: yooouuu cunt. The next time you meet an Aussie, ask him or her to say it. It's perfect; they have really perfected it. They should be commended. When they say it, it takes about a half a second longer to say it. Good day, good day, Sheila. It's a thing of beauty, almost poetic. Ya little beauty. Cheers, cunts! Tip your bartender!

TWENTY-FOUR

Wednesday, June 7, 2006
Old People

We get older people in the bar from time to time. I love talking to older people and spending time with them. They're full of knowledge and life lessons. We are all getting older, that's for sure—even me!

I recently found a gray pubic hair. Don't worry, Smithy, it wasn't mine.

I love the fact that old people say what they want. The world would be so much funnier if we were all like that. The filter seems to come off at about seventy. Is it the fact that they got to seventy and now neither give a fuck nor care what you think? If I could get a boner from old people, I would spend an awful lot more time with them.

We had the monthly chess meeting in the back room of the bar tonight. They are all older people and pretty dull, to be honest with you. They have dinner and then play chess. Woo-hoo, how exciting. It takes them two hours to pass the salt. Actually, I'm only kidding—they're great fun.

Smithy, I got chatting to this lovely couple who have been married for over fifty-five years. Can ya fuckin' Adam and Eve it? I ask them, "What's the secret to being together for so long?" The man says, "It's like this: There are two types of decisions—small ones and big ones. We decided that my wife would make all the small decisions and I would make all the big decisions. Well," he says, "there's been no big decision." Now, that's brilliant, Smithy, isn't it?

Mind you, he's the same man who also told me later in the night (after a few)—"Marriage is like a deck of cards. In the beginning all you need are two hearts and a diamond. By the end you wish you had a club and a spade." Some advice is better than others!

You know you're getting old when you fall and nobody laughs. When you hurt yourself sleeping. When the candles on your birthday cake cost more than the cake. These people are so old that they remember when Elvis was alive the first time.

You know you're getting old when your toes outnumber your teeth (that could be a west of Ireland or a Southern redneck joke, too). You are getting old when you enjoy remembering things rather than doing them—I'm not quite there yet.

Old people shouldn't eat health food; they need all the preservatives they can get.

This guy from the chess club said he went to give blood, and they told him his blood type was discontinued. The same guy said he remembered when casual sex meant no tie on. When safe sex was having the handbrake on in the car. His birth certificate was carved in stone. I asked him how he got to be so old. He said, "Cold? I'm not cold." He was old, Smithy.

Speaking of age, if you're over forty years of age and have an earring and a ponytail, you'd better be a fuckin' pirate or Keith Richards!

Well, I'm on my way home tonight in a taxi. It's lashing rain. On my way back from O'Flaherty's Bar on Forty-Sixth Street. Great after-hours place. We're heading down Ninth Avenue when the taxi skids and crashes into the back of another taxi. Well, this midget comes running out of the taxi that we just ran into, all pissed off. My taxi driver says to the little dwarf, "Which one are you?" He says, "Well, I'm not happy."

Talking about midgets and dwarfs, did you hear about the gay midget? He came out of the cupboard. I used to date a midget—I was nuts over her. I'd better quit after that one, mate.

Cheers for now, Smithy, and remember to tip your bartender!

Sunday, September 17, 2006
If the Guinness Is Good . . .

I go down to see Bazza today. Remember my mate who bartends around the corner? He's quite the character, as you know. A bleedin' header! We start talking about what makes the Guinness good, like the pour, type of glass, and the temperature, and then where the best pints of Guinness are in the city. Swift on East Fourth, The Scratcher on East Fifth, Puck Fair on Lafayette, Four-Faced Liar on West Fourth, Scallywag's on Ninth, and The Ear Inn on Spring—we agree on them.

You know how Guinness drinkers are—they will pass ten bars until they get to the pub with the better Guinness.

Then I say, "If the Guinness is good, I would drink it out of my shoe." "Bet you one hundred dollars you wouldn't," he says. "You're on."

I should have looked down to see what kind of footwear I was wearing before I agreed to the bet. Unfortunately for me, today's footwear are my blue, twelve-hole Doc Martens. Wish I were wearing sandals. But a bet's a bet. I take one off and hand it over. Sure enough, he goes through all the steps to pour a Guinness. Even puts a shamrock on top, even though he knows I hate them, cheeky cunt. The great thing about Doc Martens is that they are waterproof—unfortunate again for me—so all the Guinness stays right in the boot. Well, here goes, and I decide to take a couple of huge gulps so as to get it over with as quickly as possible. Like a Band-Aid, just rip it off and get it over with. I take the first mouthful and almost gag and puke right away. Everyone is laughing. It's basically drink, gag, drink and gag, and I eventually get it down along with some indescribable stuff and win my hundred-dollar bet. The things you do for a bet!

Then a bunch of customers come in; they look like tourists with their maps and cameras. They walk up to the taps at the bar and ask Bazza what he has on draft. "Are you fuckin' blind?" he says as he steps back and opens his arms right out to display the three taps that are in front of them—like he is selling a car or something. "Are ya fuckin' blind? You're standing right in front of them, for fuck's sake," he says again. He's a little rough around the edges, you might say. They order a couple of Belgian blonde ales, and then he says to them, "Why you cunts wanta drink that crap anyway? Here, have some Buds," and he slides them a couple of Buds across the bar. They all just seem to be in shock and pick them up and walk away to sit at a table in the corner of the bar. He's bleedin' hilarious. He's one of these guys who you need to warm up to. He can really be brutal, but he says it in a way that you can't help but laugh. About a half hour passes and Bazza walks over to them and asks them how they're doing and where they're from. "We're from Belgium," the older one says, and we all just crack up laughing, especially Bazza. It turns out it's one of their birthdays, so Bazza goes back and gets them another round, saying, "Your one is on the house. The rest of you I'm going to overcharge."

Oh my God, Smithy, it's like a comedy show when Bazza works, and you know what? By the end of it all, everyone loves him.

When you're in town, we'll stop in to see him, but whatever you do, don't order the Belgian blonde ale!

Saturday, November 25, 2006
No Smoking, Please

As we all know, you can't smoke in bars in New York City anymore. I personally think it's a good idea, but I can understand how you smokers might get pissed off. That's actually what happened when I said that to this man at the bar. Here's what happened:

I smell smoke at the bar one night, and then I notice this man smoking. It happens from time to time when people have just forgotten that they can't smoke in bars anymore. Normally when I say, "Sorry, mate, you need to bring that outside," they usually jump up apologizing and run outside—not this time. I say to this man, "You need to take that outside." He starts screaming, "Who the fuck says I can't smoke in the bar?" I say, "Relax, it's the law. Nothing we can do about it. You have to smoke outside." Again he screams, "Who the fuck says I can't smoke in this bar?" Now at this stage the whole bar has stopped and is listening to all this. I'm thinking I need to try and calm this headbanger down. "I'm sorry," I say, "there's nothing I can do about it." With this he jumps up, starts running around, screaming, "Who's gonna tell me I can't smoke in here?" Did I tell you he was a big fucker? Then I see him running around the end of the bar to try and come behind at me. He turns around the corner and enters the bar running at me. I'm like, "Relax, calm down, would ya?" He is now trying to get his hands around my neck. I'm trying to force his hands back away from my neck when he slaps me in the face. I give him a headbutt (Glasgow Kiss—that one was for you, Stevie). He falls back slightly, but it really doesn't faze him. He launches at me again, trying to get his hands back around my neck. I think I just made him mad. I think the people at the bar are in shock of what's going on and are frozen to their seats. I give him one last heave backward and reach down and grab a vodka bottle from the speed rack, and just as he steps back toward me, I crack him across the head, and he finally goes down. He's obviously drunk, so I had a huge advantage. It was all over in about ten seconds. (Mind ya, it felt like an eternity when it was happening.) The locals at the bar *now* help me get him out, and we drag him around the corner and leave him behind the back of the Cheyenne Diner in the rubbish. Four of us, each with an arm or a leg. So hopefully when he wakes up he will not come back in. I don't blame them for initially not helping me, considering how quickly it happened. We all walk back into the bar to a huge hooray and applause. He didn't come back.

Here's a better smoking story: These two older ladies were smoking outside the bar one night when it started to rain. One lady pulled out a condom from her bag, cut the end of it off, and rolled it over the cigarette, kinda like a cigarette raincoat. The lady beside her was amazed with this new invention. She says to the other lady, "How can I get one of those things?" The other lady says, "Just go down to the local drugstore and ask them for a packet of condoms."

Sure enough, the lady goes into the pharmacy the next day and says, "Can I have a packet of condoms, please?" The pharmacist says, "Sure, what kind and size do you want?" The lady, looking a little puzzled, says, "I'm not really sure . . . one that fits over a Camel?"

By the way, how many condoms can you get out of a rubber tire? 365 . . . if it's a Goodyear.

TWENTY-FIVE

Friday, May 18, 2007
The Ninth Avenue Food Festival

So it's that time of the year again—time for the Ninth Avenue Food Festival. It's the first and probably the best street fair of the year. This happens every year on the third weekend in May or the weekend after Mother's Day. Starts at Thirty-Seventh Street and Ninth Avenue and goes up Ninth Avenue all the way to Fifty-Seventh Street. I'm off on the weekends, so I always like to go. It's really a great social event as you stroll up the avenue, bumping into and catching up with friends from the neighborhood. The bar I work in is close by, so we normally start there and just saunter up the avenue. We have yet to make it all the way up, as there are a few distractions along the way. We usually stop at Manganaro's Italian deli on Thirty-Seventh Street for some abuse—great sandwiches, but known by the locals as the sandwich Nazis. Then we head up to Sea Breeze Fish Store on Fortieth for some calamari and octopus. At the start of any good session or roll, it is vital that you get some grub in your stomach.

As I said earlier, we have yet to make it all the way to the end at Fifty-Seventh Street, as there are just so many bars along the way. Maybe this will be the year—ya right, who am I kidding? Start at the Holland Bar at Thirty-Ninth Street, one of the smallest bars in the city—a real New York City institution and dive bar. Ask for Doctor Bill, the bartender; he also is the weekend bartender in my bar. He will fix you up nicely. Daltons on Forty-Third, a large comfortable bar with lots of beers on tap. Ask for Paul, the owner; tell him I sent you. Rudy's on Forty-Fourth, just look for the pig outside—another real NYC dive bar, probably the king of them. The beers are cheap, free hot dogs, great jukebox, and they have a garden in the back. Well, when I say a garden, it's a NYC garden—all concrete, full of pigeons, and no grass, unless you want to bring your own. Next is the Film Center Café bar also on Forty-Fourth—a wee bit classier then Rudy's, with good food. If you like wine, then stop in to Riposo Wine Bar on Forty-Sixth. It's a small, intimate place with great knowledgeable bartenders. (Tip: The next time you go to a wine bar and want some respect, stick your pinky out and say, "I don't love it," after you try some wine. Try it—I'm telling you, it works.)

Another of my favorites is Valhalla on Fifty-Third. This place has over thirty beers on tap, so there is something for everybody here. Then also on Fifty-Third you have Bar Nine, a lounge-style bar with couches and live music—a great place to relax and end the day.

Smithy, I love living in Hell's Kitchen, particularly the Ninth Avenue area. It's funny, people say to me all the time (including yourself), "How do you deal with all the people in NYC?" Well, I tell them I live in a village in NYC. I think that's how you survive in this city. You get to know the few blocks around where you live. If you try to take it all in at once, you will get swallowed up in the crowd. Get to know the few blocks around where you live. That was great advice I got when I first moved into the neighborhood. When I go out to shop, for instance, I see the same people as if I were in a wee town in Ireland. For instance, I go to Esposito's butcher shop for my meat on Ninth Avenue and Thirty-Eighth Street. Sea Breeze for my fish on Fortieth Street. International Foods on Fortieth for my nuts and spices, and Stiles Farmers Market (under the tent) on Forty-First for my fruit and veggies. I can get everything I need, Smithy. When all my shopping is done, I treat myself to the best cup of Joe in the city and go in to see Mike at the Cupcake Café on Fortieth Street. I'm telling you, Smithy, they have the greatest cappuccino in town, not to mention the cupcakes.

All this, Smithy, within three blocks of each other—the last great local neighborhood in Manhattan that sits in the shadows of the Port Authority Bus Station. I like it like that. There you have it: my little village in NYC.

So wherever you go on Ninth Avenue in Hell's Kitchen, you are sure to find something for everyone. Hope to see you out there.

Cheers, enjoy, and please don't forget to tip your bartenders.

Monday, June 4, 2007
Georgie Boy!

George comes in tonight. Remember the slow lad from the neighborhood I was telling you about? God bless him. He's not "retarded," per se. He's like a combination of Forrest Gump and Rain Man. Intelligent in many ways, but his social skills are lacking. He's very naïve and nervous, like an eleven-year-old boy in a thirty-something body. I like him a lot, and I always try to look out for him. He always orders a Pepsi, sits in the corner, and loves to watch sports. Yankees, Mets, Giants, and Jets—he loves them all.

When he started coming in a few years back, I was guilty myself of not really making him feel welcome. He just seemed odd, and unfortunately, like most people, I didn't give him the welcome he deserved. However, the more I talked to him, the more I enjoyed him. I just wish I had warmed up to him sooner.

George can tell you every football, basketball, and baseball result. Every player's statistics, number, and so on.

But when a woman sits beside him or near him, you can see he gets very uncomfortable. You can feel his discomfort. He freezes up and just goes into himself. Puts his head down and goes back to reading the sports section of the newspaper.

We are all talking one night, the lads, about women and somebody's last conquest. George is giggling, blushing, and sort of ducking his head down. I say to him, "George, you got a girlfriend?" "A girlfriend, n–no, never had a girlfriend," he says. "Have you ever kissed a girl?" I ask him. "N–not yet." He giggles, becoming embarrassed. "But I would like to."

I say to myself, *I think George is a virgin. Maybe I should introduce George to Pepsi. He already drinks it.*

Well, a few weeks pass and I see Pepsi one night. Remember Pepsi, the hooker? I explain George's situation and ask her if she wouldn't mind meeting him one night at the bar. She's not that excited about it, but she says she will do it anyway. She is a professional, after all.

I arrange a night for Pepsi to come in when I know George will be there as well. Pepsi walks in and I nod to her where George is sitting. She walks over and sits down next to George. I can see George is starting to get uncomfortable as I walk down to them both. "Hey, Pepsi, how're things tonight? Hey, George, this is my good friend Pepsi," I say. "N–nice to m-meet you, Pep–Pepsi," George says. "Very nice to meet you, George," Pepsi says. I gotta give it up to Pepsi; she's a real pro and knows how to put people at ease, no matter their experience level. I gained a lot of respect for her that night. I bring her down a dirty Grey Goose martini, her usual. As I'm putting it on the bar in front of her, I overhear George saying, "Pepsi—that's what I drink," as Pepsi smiles. I tell George and Pepsi that the drinks are on the house.

I walk away and serve a few more people. As I'm taking a beer out of the cooler, I hear the front door opening. Next thing I know, Pepsi and George are out the door, having left their drinks on the bar. Fuck, that was quick. Maybe George is not as slow as he makes out.

The whole rendezvous was shorter than a Tyson fight back in his prime. George left as a thirty-three-year-old boy and came back ten minutes later as a thirty-three-year-old boy, but standing up a little taller than before. "Th–thanks," George says, as he gulps down his second Pepsi that night. "Thanks a lot, I really n–needed that . . . . How are the Yanks doing?"

Thursday, July 5, 2007
Drinks

According to a recent study, scientists believe that coffee can reduce the effects of alcohol on the liver. They say that two cups of coffee a day can as much as halve the effects on the liver. Today Charlie Sheen crashed into a Starbucks. I was in Starbucks today and some lady ordered a decaffeinated espresso. Is that an oxymoron or what, Smithy? Like deafening silence, original copy, seriously funny, and clearly confused. I was clearly confused. That's like going in to a chemist and asking for non-drowsy sleeping pills—what's the bleedin' point?

The new crazes in the bars now are these big shots—the ones that you drop a shot into a pint of something. People love car bombs (half pint of Guinness and a half shot of Bailey's and Irish whiskey). Then there's Jager bombs (half pint of Red Bull and a shot of Jager). Drop the shot into the pint and chug away. What a combination. Pissed drunk and awake. They all sound terrible, but they're gooood.

When did a vodka and cranberry turn into a cranberry and vodka? You can tell the age of somebody by how they order. The young ones order cranberry and vodka—and they order one drink at a time. I will come back with the cranberry and vodka, and then she or her friend will say, "Can I have a cranberry and vodka?" You know what, girls, making two or three at a time is a lot easier and quicker for me. You will never hear an old lady order it that way. It's like asking for jelly and peanut butter. It's always been a peanut butter and jelly sandwich, and it always will be. Just as it will always be a vodka and cranberry. Stop fucking with the drink-ordering process, people.

By the way, have you noticed that beer is now cheaper than gas? So drink but don't drive.

This man walked into the bar last night and asked me for a pint of water. Then he asked me if I could fill the last part with beer. I say, "That's an unusual drink request." He says, "You'd order it if you had what I have."

"What do you have?" I say. He says, "A quarter." That's weird, right, Smithy?

We get people coming in from time to time selling roses for the romantics at the bar, hoping they will buy them for their wives or girlfriends. I was out with the girlfriend the other night, and one of these lads came by selling roses. He came up to me and asked me if I wanted to buy a rose for, as he put it, "The lovely lady." I informed him that I didn't need to buy one as I had already slept with her! And what about the man? When are we going to have people coming around selling hammers and drills for women to buy for their boyfriends and husbands? It's just not fair, is it?

Well, Smithy, talk to you later, and remember to tip your bartenders!

TWENTY-SIX

Saturday, August 18, 2007
New Yorkers and Their Pets

As we all know, New Yorkers love their pets. Once in a while we have people come in with their pets. Dogs, cats, gerbils (we are very close to Chelsea, after all), and so on.

This rabbi came in the bar with a frog on his shoulder. I said to him, "Where did you get that?" The frog said, "Brooklyn. There's fuckin' loads of them."

For me the only pets I can handle right now are goldfish. I named my goldfish Number One and Number Two. When one died, I still had two!

When it gets slow late at night and the kitchen is closed, I don't mind when the locals bring in their dogs. I actually enjoy the dogs. This one fella—let's call him Martin—comes in at nights with his dogs. He goes out every night to walk his dogs and pops into the bar and has at least three or four shots of vodka. Then he goes home to the wife—he always walks his dogs. He was telling me one time that he had to leave town unexpectedly, so his wife had to walk the dogs. So she is walking the dogs, and as they go by the bar the dogs make a right and head straight for the front door of the bar, all excited and barking for us to open the door. The dogs ratted him out. No more late-night dog walking for Martin.

Another time this fella says to a man who has this dog sitting under his table, "Does your dog bite?" "No," he says. The fella goes to stroke the dog on the back. Just as he does, the dog takes a big bite out of his arm. The fella screams and shouts at the guy, "I thought you said your dog doesn't bite?" "That's not my dog," he says.

Another time this man says, "Is that a Jack Russell?" "No," the other guy says, "it's mine."

Stevie Wonder came into the bar one night with his dog. Picked his dog up by the tail and started swinging it around his head. I say to him, "Stevie, what the fuck are you doing?" He says, "Relax, I'm just having a look around!" Did you ever see his wife? Neither has he.

He told me that he recently got a cheese grater for his birthday. He said it's the best book he has ever read! I believe he recently got divorced. Guess he didn't see that coming either. His estate was split 50/50. I'm sure he would have preferred 20/20.

People, please stop decorating your dogs. Stop putting these ridiculous outfits on your dogs. They are so embarrassed. And, by the way, they are already wearing a coat. They are born with one already on, you stupid fuckers. Let dogs be dogs. Stop trying to humanize animals. All your dog wants to do is lick his balls, but he can't because he's got a jacket and a pair of trousers on. Like the very old joke goes, why do dogs lick their balls? Because they can.

That reminds me, this is for all the men. If you're on a date, don't get a doggy bag. It makes you look like a little pussy. While you're at it, you may as well get your balls and put them in a doggy bag because you won't be needing them that night . . . and you're welcome.

Now go out and get yourself a nice cold beer and remember to tip your bartender! Cheers, Smithy.

Wednesday, September 5, 2007
A Real New Yorker!

It's official, Smithy. I'm now a "real" New Yorker, well, according to the regulars at the bar anyway. I came in to work tonight explaining that I had just killed a cockroach with my bare hands in my apartment. Next thing one of the locals stands up and says, "Listen up, everybody, I would like to say (pointing at me) he has officially become a New Yorker today!" He went on to retell my cockroach story. Apparently that is one of the many scenarios involved in becoming a real New Yorker—killing a cockroach with your bare hands. Then everyone at the bar started chirping in with their own reasons why they were a real New Yorker. Quite funny.

You are a real New Yorker when: You know the quickest way to get to anywhere in New York City, either by subway, bus, taxi, or walking. You know exactly which door to get on the subway so it lets you off at the stairway of your next stop. When you've been on the Cyclone in Coney Island more than ten times. Had a dirty dog. Driven a pedicab. Know how to get cheap or free tickets for Broadway. Have seen Woody Allen for the second time. (Seeing him for the first time—not good enough.) Can get into the Central Park Zoo for free. Had an egg float. Stolen a cab from somebody who was ahead of you. Ridden the Staten Island Ferry on an afternoon off. Know brassers (prostitutes) on a first-name basis. Had pizza at Grimaldi's, Lombardi's, or my favorite, Arturo's. Have been kicked out of at least one public library or museum. (You know that most NYC museums are technically free.) Been to the MET thirty-seven times. Know "Smokey" in Central Park. Been in the Mermaid Parade. Have met Jimmy at Jimmy's Corner Bar. Shouted randomly at anybody on the street. Had a pastrami sandwich at Katz's Deli or the Second Avenue Deli— when it was on Second Avenue. Have sung karaoke at Sing Sing. Hung out at 7B. "Hated" Tavern on the Green. Given a tourist the "wrong" directions on purpose. (Now that's just mean!) Kicked a taxi cab. Remember Mars Bar (a bar where you wiped your feet on the way out) and CBGB's. Had a burger at Corner Bistro. Can understand the subway announcements.

Well, there you have it, Smithy. That's *all* it takes to become a real New Yorker!

TWENTY-SEVEN

Monday, September 24, 2007
Heading to Amsterdam for a Week

You know my mate Joe, the mad fucker—he's as mad as a brush but a great lad. Well, he's getting married—never saw that one coming! I suppose you have to get married sometime; you can't live your whole life being happy! A few of us have decided to go to Amsterdam for the bachelor party. Is there a better place to spend your last few single days than the Dam? I think not.

So we're on the plane, and the stewardess is doing the how-to-buckle-your-seat-belt demonstration, when Joe stands up and says, "Any chance of a drink, luv?" They don't like this generally, I find. She stops what she is doing and says, "Excuse me, sir, but we are not serving drinks right now. Please sit down." "Okay, luv, let me know when you are; I'm dying for one, right," Joe replies.

We are now some forty thousand feet in the air, rocketing to a foreign country, when Joe decides to go into the toilet to smoke a joint. I don't even want to know how he got the joint on the plane—not to mention why! I mean, come on, who smuggles weed into Amsterdam? I told you he was bleedin' mad, Smithy.

Anyway, as he is coming out of the toilet, the flight attendant just so happens to be walking by at the exact same time, and she smells what he leaves behind, not to mention the cloud of smoke that preceded him—like a rock star coming on stage. The flight attendant goes berserk and informs Joe that he will be arrested when we land, to which Joe starts to giggle—not helping the situation. I guess the weed must have been kickin' in. Steve and I say how sorry we are—that it's his first time on a plane and we're really just trying our best to resolve the situation. She's having none of it.

A few hours pass, and after many more attempts to try and soften her up, she leans over the three of us just as we are about to descend into Amsterdam, smiles, and says, "Enjoy Amsterdam. Don't do anything I wouldn't do," winks, and walks away. Thank fuck for that; what a darling. That holiday coulda gotten off to a bad start.

We get off the plane, leave the airport, and get onto the train to the center of Amsterdam as quickly as possible, just in case she had a change of heart. Check into the Hotel Metro, shower up, and go out to the Grasshopper Bar for our first night in Amsterdam.

Another of the many delights about Amsterdam are all the kebab shops—a big favorite of ours, as you know, Smithy. The Irish love their kebabs. I'm not talking about your generic abracadabras that are on every corner in Ireland. The ones over there are the real McCoy—the mecca of the kebab world. It wasn't long before we found ourselves outside one, as there was one conveniently across the street. We tossed coins—actually, beer mats—to see who would go for kebabs, and Joe lost. He had been pretty lucky so far today; maybe he'd used it all up. He had been a jammy bastard.

Before I was halfway through my kebab, Joe had finished, downing his in four aggressive mouthfuls. "I love kebabs. I could eat two for every meal," Joe declared, wiping garlic sauce off his chin with his hands. "No way," I said. "Could so. I could do it easily!"

Okay then. "I bet you can't eat two kebabs per meal between now and the end of the week. That's seven days at six a day . . . that's forty-two kebabs," I challenged. "Too easy," he countered. "For a hundred dollars." "You're on," I told him, but under my breath I said, "You're going to need the hundred dollars if you survive—for the hospital bill." Done. We shook on it as Joe stood up and approached the kiosk again. I would win this bet for sure, and Joe would learn a valuable lesson in thinking before speaking. It's a win-win situation. "Two kebabs, thanks!" Joe ordered for himself. He was going down fighting, I'll give him that. And go down he would go.

It is unseasonably hot in Amsterdam for this time of the year. Joe benefited the most, as he has managed to sweat out the majority of the kebabs he has eaten so far. It's the third day, so that means roughly about eighteen kebabs so far.

After the kebab breakfast (Joe has his customary two or three kebabs), we head to the coffee shops. The bulldog. The only culture we have seen so far. Fuck the Anne Frank, Rembrandt, or Van Gogh museums. We head straight to the pub. Now, Smithy, they're not your usual pubs; they're called coffee shops—not too much coffee drunk in these places, mind ya. The lad behind the counter gives us a menu—for weed. Can you fuckin' Adam and Eve it? A bloody menu for weed! Wow, what should I order? Spoiled for choice. I ask the fellow, "What would you recommend?" He says, "Do you want to be happy, sad, up, or down, semiconscious, conscious, freaked out, not so freaked out, paranoid as fuck," and so on—ya get my point. I settle on the white widow from Afghanistan. Now here comes the fun part. The lad behind the counter puts all the smoke from the weed into a vaporizer. Never had one before. Was he going to smoke it for us as well? A vaporizer is condensed pure weed—no smoke. Fuck, it's good, Smithy.

Before I know it, the hallucinations begin and I think I'm some kind of a superhero. I grab the cloth off the table beside us (glasses and plates still on top of it) and swoosh out the door (well, that's what they told me)—destination unknown. Long story painful, I wake up on a barge several hours later on the canal. They said that I went out so quickly they never had a chance to catch up with me. The excitement got the better of me. Need to dial it down a bit.

Next morning I'm feeling a bit rough, but not as rough as Joe, who is in serious pain in the toilet. I think the thirty kebabs are finally fighting back. Steve and I decide to explore Amsterdam by ourselves and get a bit of culture. It was actually good to just do our own thing for a while.

I head to the Anne Frank house in the center of Amsterdam at Prinsen-gracht. It was probably about time I got out of the coffee shops and experienced more culture in Amsterdam.

I finally get to the Anne Frank house after almost getting run over by the many cyclists in the city. I figured it was free, like most of the museums in New York, so I just walk right in and head up the stairs, walking by about ten people. Then I notice the girl behind the booth start to follow me up the stairs, saying something in Dutch, I assume. She's looking for me, but I'm already on the third floor. I can see her as I look down between the stairs. Now I feel a little embarrassed, so I decide to hide behind this bookcase. I didn't know where else to go. She was looking for me for about an hour, so I decided to keep a diary about my adventure. "Thursday, in the Anne Frank house, I didn't know I had to pay to get into the Anne Frank house, smaller than I pictured, love the canals and the cobblestone streets, watch out for the cyclists, fuck, the weed is good in Amsterdam, and now I'm hiding behind a bookshelf." I decided to leave the diary there when I fled. Hope somebody finds it and learns about Amsterdam and that you have to pay to get into the Anne Frank house. That's enough culture for today. Next stop: coffee shop.

Well, anyway, after about four or five days of playing cards, drinking, and smoking pot, we're starting to get a wee bit bored. Most of us still haven't seen a glimpse of a Rembrandt or a . . . .

Joe is feeling better and back on the kebabs. He has a completely genius idea that we play for hookers. Cards, that is. So Steve and I say, "Let's get it straight, whoever wins the card game, the other two have to pay for the hook-er." "Yup," Joe says. "That's grand," says Steve. I'm like, "That seems too easy and not very painful. How about this: whoever loses, the other two pay for the hooker?" "Oh, for fuck's sake, sure that's easy. Everyone will want to lose," Joe says. I'm like, "Well, wait, I'm not finished. Whoever loses, the other two have to pay for the hooker. However, the hooker has to be the ugliest (plainest-looking—for political correctness, people) hooker that there is on the strip. I'm talking old, worn-out, rowdy-looking." We all agree to do it!

So Joe loses the first night at cards, and I already have in mind a hooker whom I noticed earlier. God bless her, she was a hideous old lady with a face like a boot. By the way, there were no buy-outs. You could not go in there and not perform, if you know what I mean. You had to get whatever we paid for, and we were paying for everything—the full monty. We were on the "honor" system (again, all pun intended). We tell Joe we will meet him around the corner in the Bulldog. Sure enough, Joe comes in about an hour later, the amount we paid for, and orders a Heineken and three shots of Jagermeister—all for him. Probably trying to get the taste out of his mouth. Steve is like, "You're the bravest man I know. Tonto . . . that's it—you're fuckin' Tonto." So Joe's new name is Tonto.

Next up: Steve. Again we walk around the Red Light District way too long looking for someone for Steve. "Na, she's too nice—not ugly enough," we say. "Let's keep going." We walk through this tunnel on the edge of the Red Light District, and as we turn the corner we see this shadow in the window. Then the red light comes on, and we see this woman with a patch over one of her eyes. No kiddin', I swear, she had a patch over her eye. Not sure which one, but does it really matter? She was an old Spanish lady with a patch over her eye. All she was missing was a parrot—perfect! Steve goes in and Zorro comes out.

I'm up next. I hate these fuckers; we musta walked around for hours until they finally settled on a monkey. I'm not trying to be funny here or disrespectful in any way, but she looked like a gorilla. About three hundred pounds, with thick, black dreadlocks down to her knees. A belly on her that would have put a seasoned Guinness drinker to shame. Honest to God, I was fuckin' scared. No, I was terrified. Well, I came out Tarzan. Enough said.

Well, there you have it, Smithy. Joe, Steve, and I went to the Dam and came back as Tonto, Zorro, and Tarzan. After a week in Amsterdam that would have made Keith Richards proud, it was time to go home—thank God.

We're on the plane home after having spent a week in Amsterdam—never saw a museum or an art gallery (except for my adventure at the Anne Frank house). We start drinking and chatting about our trip. So Steve, a.k.a. Zorro, says to me, a.k.a. Tarzan, "Did you really shag that bird?" "Actually, I got to be honest with ya, I could not do it," I say. Steve says, "I couldn't do it either." Joe, a.k.a. Tonto, turns to me and Steve and says, "You bastards! I shagged mine."

Well, we all just crack up laughing. So much for the honor system. Well, except for Joe. He is the bravest man I know, after all.

TWENTY-EIGHT

Monday, October 8, 2007
The New York Yankees

Three baseball fans were on their way to a game when one noticed a foot sticking out of the bushes by the side of the road. They stopped and discovered a nude female, dead drunk. Out of respect and propriety, the New York Yankees fan took off his cap and placed it over her right breast. The Chicago Cubs fan took off his cap and placed it over her left breast. Following their lead, but with some grumbling, the Boston Red Sox fan took off his cap and placed it over her crotch. The police were called, and when the officer arrived, he conducted his inspection. First, he lifted the Yankees cap, replaced it, and wrote down some notes. Next he lifted the Cubs cap, replaced it, and wrote down some notes. The officer then lifted the Red Sox cap, replaced it, then lifted it again, replaced it, lifted it a third time, and replaced it one last time. The Red Sox fan was getting upset and finally asked, "What are you, some kind of a pervert? Why do you keep lifting and looking?" "Well," said the officer, "I am simply surprised. Normally when I look under a Red Sox cap, I find an arsehole!"

Went to the New York Yankees baseball game today. Took the D train right to Yankee stadium—very convenient from where I live. I got to talking with this man seated beside me at the game—nice fella. I noticed beside him was an empty seat. I said to him, "It's unusual to see an empty seat at a Yankees game, isn't it?" He replied, "I bought it for my wife, but she died." I said to him, "I am very sorry, but could you not have given it to one of your friends or family members?" He said, "They're actually a very strange bunch. They're all at the funeral." Talk about a die-hard Yankee fan!

I went with my girlfriend to the game today. I kissed her between the strikes and she kissed me between the balls.

The New York Yankees lost in the first round of the baseball playoffs to the

Cleveland Indians. The Yankees and their fans are obviously very sad and disappointed, as am I, but not as sad as the Cleveland Indians, as now they have to go back to Cleveland.

Why do Mets fans hate the Yankees so much? I was working behind the bar during the Yankees-Indians series and there were about twenty guys at the end of the bar. They were all routing for the Cleveland Indians. I say to them, "Are you all from Cleveland?" They say, "No, we're from Sunnyside, Queens." What a bunch of jealous wankers. Wouldn't you think if you were from Queens, New York, you would root for your local New York team against a bunch of fuckin' Indians?

There's this Met fan who can't stop masturbating. He goes to the doctor and says, "Every time I finish masturbating I sing the Mets song." The doctor says, "Don't worry, thousands of wankers sing that song." See you next season, losers!

The Edge, the lead guitar player for the band U2, donated his 1975 Gibson guitar to the New Orleans hurricane disaster fund today. He said he wanted to give away something that he would miss. "How about your house?" the people of New Orleans said.

That reminds me, Bono was doing a concert in his hometown of Dublin recently and started clapping his hands and saying to the crowd, "Every time I clap my hands a person in Africa dies." Somebody shouted up from the crowd, "Well, Bono, stop clapping your fucking hands then."

He recently fell off the stage at Croke Park, in Dublin. He fell over the Edge!

Thursday, October 11, 2007
I Swear You Can't Make This Shite Up!

I was telling these people in the bar one day how in Ireland the fish, particularly the salmon, are jumping out of the water—literally. There are just so many of them. There is actually one place in County Kerry where if you lean over this bridge as the salmon are coming up the river, you can actually grab them out of the air as they jump out of the water. These two Polish guys overhear my conversation and tell me they are actually going to Ireland to see family next week, and they will go and try to catch some salmon. I tell them exactly where this place is in Kerry. They leave and tell me they will be back in the bar in a few weeks and will tell me what happened.

Sure enough, a few weeks go by and these two Polish guys come back into the bar. Here's their story; it's priceless.

So we get to County Kerry in Ireland, and we locate the bridge where the salmon are supposed to be. I lean over the bridge while my friend holds my feet so I can get down low. Just as you told us.

After about an hour my friend starts screaming and shouting, "Pull me up! Pull me up!" I say to him, "Did you get a salmon?" "No," he says. "There's a train coming."

As I said earlier you can't make this shite up.

TWENTY-NINE

Monday, October 15, 2007
I'm a Little Sad :(

just broke up with the girlfriend. When will I learn? She told me I wasn't very considerate to her needs. I don't understand why she would say that. Actually, I haven't told her yet—gonna send her a text later. Actually, an ex-girlfriend of mine came into the bar tonight looking all hot and sexy, but my rule is simple: there's only one reason to go back with an ex-girlfriend—breast implants. (Or should I say two reasons!)

Honesty is really the key to a good and healthy relationship. And if you can fake that, you're laughing.

I think the Irish are known to stretch the truth a wee bit. Fib a bit—make shite up. None of these stories, of course! We all do in Ireland. I've made myself so much more interesting. As you know, Smithy, growing up in a dreary place like Dublin, we need to spice it up a bit. It's much more fun that way. What do they say? "The truth will set you free," but the lies are so much more fun. It's not that people don't like being lied to; it's just that they don't like it when they find out!

I don't know, Smithy, do you think the Irish are affectionate and emotional? I'm not sure. Sometimes we are and sometimes we're not. I know that's the case with me. I suppose a lot of these feelings originate from our parents. I think most of our parents didn't grow up in a very emotional era—at least the "I love you" era. I love you—what's that? Don't think they heard that too often.

My girlfriend used to say to me, "You remind me of the ocean." I would say, "Wet and wild." "No," she would say. "You make me fuckin' sick."

We used to hold hands a lot—because if we had ever let go, we would have probably fuckin' killed each other. It was a good breakup as breakups go. For instance, we split the apartment in New York City in half—she got the inside.

I won't mention the cat. The good thing about being married or being in a relationship is that when you go home, there is somebody there; the bad thing about being married or in a relationship is that when you go home, there is somebody there!

Relationships are hard, as we all know. There are two types of relationships that don't work: long distance and short distance. You need to find a happy medium.

I met this older lady not too long ago who was recently divorced. They call them cougars over here.

We're out one night and she tells me that she hasn't been out on a date in twenty years. She says, "What's it like out there dating these days?" "Things have changed a wee bit," I say. "First of all, the woman always pays for dinner, and second, sex is a given." "I'm definitely not paying for dinner," she says.

She told me that people actually advised her not to go out with me. "Well, it worked for Romeo and Juliet," I said. Of course, minus the stabbing and poisoning. The only thing I don't like about older women—particularly, I'm sure, in NYC—is all this plastic surgery. Come on, ladies—don't do it. Stop reading all the glamour magazines and listening to and paying attention to what society and social norms tell you how you should look. Do you want to look like you're forty-five or do you want to look like a lizard? Let it go—age gracefully! There's nothing as beautiful as an older lady who is comfortable in her own skin.

You know how old they are by the amount of times they get up to go to the bathroom. You can lie all you want about your age, but your bladder can't.

I'm really starting to enjoy dating older people—cougars. They're usually a lot more mature. Considering I'm not, that really helps. And they go home after sex. They don't lie there like a lovesick puppy.

All joking aside, Smithy, relationships are probably the hardest thing in the world to figure out. We are all in relationships—whether it's with your postman or your partner. I have had many relationships with people, but once feelings come into them, they change. I enjoy being in relationships, and obviously I'm no expert—far from it. I enjoy being in love. I believe in love. Love excites me. I cannot explain it, and I don't want to explain it. It's love. You know when you are in love. You don't need to explain how you feel or why you feel like that. Sometimes it's better not to explain. But every journey ends!

I want to believe in love . . . again. I don't want to be afraid to love again, and I don't want to run away from all the brilliant possibilities of life.

Being in a relationship with a bartender must be difficult. Not being home five nights a week can be stressful on a relationship—no doubt. Sneaking in beside your partner so as not to wake her. Then moments later it seems she's getting up for the day. Me sleeping half the day away.

Maybe she had already left before I realized. Or maybe she was talking too loud for me to hear her. Relationships and people are not numbers. They're more like letters—those letters all wanting to tell a story. Unique stories. All collectively important and vital for us to get up each day. A story that is worth hearing and sharing. I suppose if relationships were easy to find, they wouldn't be worth finding. It's not about what happened before or what's going to happen next. It's about now—today. Maybe if you believe in something magical, then maybe something magical will happen. Don't cry because it's over—smile because it happened. I think you need to go through these things and times in life in order to become a better person. But you need to let go of the past in order to have a future. A relationship in which you can really make a moment out of yours and somebody else's life! Find the song in your life. Bend all the forks that you want. I hope one day someone special will walk into my life and allow me to see why it never worked out with anyone else . . . .

I remember dating this one girl who used to love to argue. Remember her, Smithy? She fuckin' adored it. If there were a career for arguing, she would have been the president. I was sleeping one night and she actually woke me up to argue, screaming at me, "I had a dream you were sleeping with somebody else, you bastard!" I said, "So did I."

Then you have the girlfriends who agree with everything you do and say, always telling you how great you are. I'm always wary of somebody who constantly tells you how great you are. They are usually looking for something. If you get a bird and she tells you, "You're a prick," hang on to her.

Well, I have been married twice, as you know, Smithy. What can I say? I love wedding cake. By the way, you know scientists have invented a food that reduces a woman's sex drive by 99 percent? It's called wedding cake. They have also discovered a chemical in women's brains that makes them talk more than men. It's called Merlot!

My first wife drowned in a wishing well. I didn't know they worked—think about it, Smithy.

No, seriously, the first wife died from eating poisoned mushrooms. The second wife died of a fractured skull—she wouldn't eat the mushrooms.

Really, my last wife died of VD. My friend said to me, "Nobody dies of VD." I said, "They do when they give it to me." She actually talked through her nose because her mouth was so worn out!

Smithy, you know the three rings of marriage: the engagement ring, the wedding ring, and the suffering!

I am actually selling a full set of Britannica encyclopedias if anyone is interested. I don't need them anymore; my girlfriend knows fuckin' everything.

I know I have a lot of growing up to do. I realized that the other day when I was playing on the swings.

I said to my girlfriend, "Were you faking it last night?" "No," she said. "I really was asleep."

A girl said to me that I don't have honest eyes. I'm like, "I just want to sleep with you, not borrow money."

I was with this girl from Scandinavia a while back. Gorgeous girl—they all are from that part of the world. She was so pretty that when you looked at her you could hear a Coldplay song. You know the type—tall, slender, and blonde. Right up my alley. I think she was from Finland, even though she kept saying, "I'm not finished; I'm not finished."

Smithy, you can't have sex with your friends. I have no more friends. When you're having sex with your friend, just remember you are losing a ride to the airport—I have to take the bus now.

I was in bed with my girlfriend the other night and she said she would like to try something different—how about the 69? I said, "You want chicken and broccoli at five o'clock in the morning?" That's the great thing about NYC—you can always find a Chinese restaurant open. We went down to Wo Hop on Mott Street in Chinatown—open twenty-four hours. You remember Nina and I went there—still no sign of her!

Seriously, Smithy, I'm actually really concerned about her. I haven't seen her in a long time, and I have no way of contacting her. My God, I hope she's all right.

Talk to you soon, mate. I will let you know if I see her.

Thursday, November 9, 2007
I Love My Neighbors

So this pretty young girl walks into the bar and asks me for a martini. I make the martini and go on doing my thing. I love making martinis, so right away I'm happy. She knows she's hot, but not much else. I have never seen her before, so I ask her if she has ever been in the bar before—just really being welcoming to her. She tells me she just moved into the high-rise building across the street. She is sitting at the end of the bar, and from our vantage point we can actually see her apartment—her exact window across the street—the fifth floor, third window from the left, as she so elegantly points out. Then she goes on to say how much she loves to walk around her apartment naked. "I never put curtains on my windows," she says, which I can already see. I think we can all see where this is going. I make a few more drinks and another martini for our new neighbor. Well, about two hours pass, a little chitchat, and she says to me, "Well, I think it's time for me to go home, take off my clothes, and call it a night. Don't forget where I live," she says, pointing up to her window across the street. I say, "Nice talking to you, luv," as I lean over the bar and give her a kiss on the cheek. "Hope to see you soon!" I'm thinking I will be seeing her very soon and very naked. I keep saying to myself, so I don't forget, *Fifth floor, third window from the left, fifth floor, third window from the left*. I'm not some kind of a pervert or peeping Tom, but come on! So sure enough, lights come on, fifth floor, third window from the left, and our new neighbor appears. She starts to do a strip tease just for me as I watch from the bar across the street.

It's getting late now, so I open up a beer—I feel it's appropriate—sit down, and enjoy the show. If I smoked I would light up. Then, have a guess what happens next, Smithy. The phone rings at the bar, and it's my new naked friend from across the street.

Last call, everybody, last call. Time to go home.

So thank you, neighbor, for the show and the lovely night, and I didn't even have to tip her, Smithy.

Tuesday, November 27, 2007
Singer John Mayer Does Comedy?

It's Sunday night, my night off from the bar, so I decided to go to the Comedy Cellar comedy club on MacDougal Street. We all got a surprise guest appearance from yours truly, John Mayer—you know, the singer. Let me tell you, Smithy, he's a better singer. He was about as funny as snot in my cup of tea. I will give him credit for getting up there and giving it a go. I went there to see one of my favorite comedians, Dave Attel, who is always funny and original. If you're in New York you have to go to the Comedy Cellar, as it's the best in the city. We had a great New York night, and only in New York can you go out to a comedy club and see a singer like John Mayer try and do stand up. I just wanted to share that story with you, and you're welcome.

I was with my girlfriend at the show, and as I said, we had a great time. We have been dating for a lil' while now, and all is good, but as we all know, dating can be tough. I remember one time dating a girl all summer long because she had air-conditioning and I didn't. Sometimes you just need to survive—you know how hot it gets in New York in the summer. I dated a cop for a while; for years the law was doing me, but then I was doing the law—I loved it. They're all hard—being married, single—you have to work on them all. It basically boils down to this: do you want to be lonely or annoyed? And whichever one you can handle the best, you should go for it. Well, as we all know, New York is not cheap, so I must get back to the bar to make some money. Cheers, Smithy, talk to ya soon.

Tuesday, December 11, 2007
O.J. Simpson—What an Arsehole!

O.J. Simpson, not happy getting away with the murder of the century, now wants to get away with burglary. Did you hear, Smithy? O.J. got arrested recently in Las Vegas for burglary. But to be fair to him, he said he was actually going there to kill someone. He actually stole his own stuff. That's like holding yourself up. What kind of dickhead gets arrested for stealing "their own stuff"? You know what O.J. stands for? "Orange jumpsuit."

What's the difference between O.J. and Adolf Hitler? Hitler left fewer clues.

O.J. would eventually be convicted and sentenced to do a minimum of nine years. Is he not the biggest dipshit in the world? He gets away with murder, and he's still not happy. If that were me—and probably the rest of the normal world—I would not spit on the street or even jaywalk. I would be the greatest citizen on the face of this earth. Well, maybe there is a God after all. He did have it coming.

Like Michael Vick, you know, the NFL quarterback who was arrested for setting up a dog-fighting game in his luxurious home in Atlanta, Georgia? He was sentenced today to almost two years in jail—actually twenty-three months—for cruelty to animals. It's funny how things work out sometimes, isn't it, Smithy, as now he will be forced to do it "doggie style" by his cellmate in prison. Don't drop the soap, Michael. Who said there was no justice in the world?

Saturday, January 12, 2008
Please Don't Throw Bar Stools at Me!

Don't throw bar stools at bartenders—please. Last night these two guys and a girl walked into the bar at about three thirty in the morning. I can see they are pretty fucked up. Now I don't want somebody else's headache, so what I usually say is, "Sorry, guys, I can't serve you; you've had too much. Come back tomorrow and I will buy you a beer. Cheers, and get home safe." This is when drunks usually say to themselves, *a free drink tomorrow sounds good,* and they leave—like they will remember about the free drink tomorrow. But this scumbag picks up a bar stool and throws it right at me. I suppose he thought I said chairs instead of cheers! I duck, and miraculously the stool misses me and lands behind me against the back bar. Again, amazingly, nothing breaks. Now I'm pissed off and I start to run around the bar to get to him. He runs out the door like the fucking coward that he is. I catch up to him about ten feet outside the door, he swings at me, I duck again for the second time, and I put him to the ground. Let's just say he will not be coming around here again. It's funny how the loudest person in the bar is usually the weakest.

The last few people who were in the bar ran out after me and pulled me off of him. He stumbled off into the night—fuckin' prick.

THIRTY

Monday, March 17, 2008
Happy Saint Patrick's Day

Well, happy Saint Patrick's Day, Smithy. Here's to the wearing of the green, kiss me I'm Irish, and all that shite. The one day of the year when every young person in New York City gets shitfaced. I actually enjoy Saint Pat's Day. It's a crazy day. Where I work, I normally work by myself, but on this day everybody works—all hands on deck. So in a way I can relax and enjoy the holiday a wee bit more as I have more help behind the bar. The music is loud and the green beer is flowing.

The Irish handcuffs—a beer in each hand.

On Saint Patrick's Day in particular, people are constantly coming up to me saying they're Irish. I suppose everybody is Irish on Saint Paddy's Day. You wouldn't believe the shite that people tell me. "I'm Irish," they say. I say, "Oh really? Where were you born in Ireland?" And, as always, the response is, "Oh, I've never been to Ireland—but I'm Irish." NO, YOU'RE NOT!

What's the fascination with being Irish? The closest they have come to Ireland or being Irish is having a pint of Guinness, a shot of Jameson, or an Irish stew. I know people like to be a part of a group—it's human nature; I understand that. However, do people realize that the Irish have been downtrodden for hundreds of years? Just read a history book. I would pick another group of people to associate with. America is a pretty good one—it's actually the best one, as I see it. I want to be a part of this group. They may have some problems, but there's a reason why millions flock to the shores of America each year and why you meet all walks of life and ethnicities in America—particularly in New York City. You're fuckin' Americans, for God's sake; be proud of it. There's a lot to be proud of, ya gobshites.

Don't get me wrong, Smithy. As you know, I'm proud to be Irish and will always be Irish, but I'm also proud to belong to America and to be an American. I tell people all the time, "Try living somewhere else for a while, and you will realize how lucky and fortunate you are to be living in America and to be an American."

Everybody seems to think that you have to be totally drunk off your arse on Saint Pat's Day. People roll into the bar all day and are usually legless. They can't even stand up, they're so drunk. In Ireland it's a religious day, and we actually take that day off, as you know. In NYC it's amateur day, and for some reason people think you need to drink like a fish. Holy shite, for fuck's sake, Smithy, it's ridiculous and embarrassing how people behave on Saint Pat's Day. And that's saying a lot coming from an Irishman.

On a sad note, two Irish guys drowned last night in the Hudson River. They believe they were trying to do the Riverdance!

People, this year can you please stop asking me if I know Pat Murphy from Dublin. I know I'm from Ireland, but there are almost six million people living in Ireland, and most of them live in Dublin. Also, please don't keep saying you would love to go to Ireland. I have this one customer who's been saying this to me for years. It's not like it's the moon—it's six hours away on a plane. It's harder to go to the Upper East Side from the West Side of Manhattan. Go to JFK Airport, book a flight, and go, shithead. You will be there in no time. Actually, by the time this ridiculously boring conversation that I'm having with you is over, you will be halfway there.

People say to me all the time: "Oh, with that accent you must get laid all the time." Actually, they're kinda right; people love an accent. However, I was not exactly a virgin when I came to New York City. So in a way, it's not a compliment; it's more like a backhanded compliment.

Like when people say "no disrespect," and then they totally disrespect you. Or "no offense," and they totally offend you. What they're actually saying is, "If you didn't have an accent, you wouldn't get laid, you ugly fucker." Thanks a lot, people.

My dad was actually born on Saint Patrick's Day, but a baby is probably more likely to be conceived on Saint Patrick's Day. Did ya know that in Chicago they dye the river green on Saint Pat's Day? In New York they don't have to. The only other times when the river in Chicago is green is when Oprah washes her money.

It's funny, on Saint Paddy's Day, usually by twelve o'clock, the night starts to quiet down. Most people start drinking so early that day that they are done early. It works for me. So by twelve o'clock, if the crowd is good, I usually lock the door and start a singsong to end the night. You don't want the drunks stumbling in after that anyway. I start it off with "Molly Malone" or "The Dublin Saunter," and we go from there. We go along the bar, and everyone has to get involved. If you don't know a song, you have to tell a joke. It's a great way to end the night.

So anyway, it's about three in the morning, and I'm starting to clean up a little bit. It's been a long day. I'm bending over to pick up some rubbish, when I get pinched on the arse. As I turn around, she (I hope it's a she) puts her two hands over my eyes. She says, "If you don't wear green on Saint Paddy's Day, you get a pinch." I say, "I'm wearing green boxers." "Well," she says, "we're going to have to see about that, now, aren't we?"

Fast-forward to the next morning. I actually wake up not knowing where I am, feeling very groggy and hung over. You know those first few seconds. Slight panic sets in until you remember how you got there. I know it's not my room because it smells . . . really nice. The walls are not crooked, and there's lovely carpeting on the floor. The room is beautiful. Curtains and lilac flowers in the corner. The bed is huge, and the silk sheets are so comforting. When I finally open up both eyes and turn around, I notice I'm alone. Where the fuck am I? Where's my date? Then I notice what looks like a very happy couple in a photo on the nightstand. I hope the fuck I'm in the guest room. I start to piece together the previous night. Okay, I remember leaving with the arse-pinching lady, getting into a cab, and going to her favorite place on the Upper East Side. That's about it. Don't remember much after that. I usually never venture up to the UES; maybe that's why my memory is foggy. Most people who live on the West Side don't go there, either. First of all, you need to transfer on the subway to get there (big no-no), and the most important reason: it's full of pretentious, yuppie snobs who wear their sweaters around their necks. It's like going to Connecticut. She must have been hot.

Then I notice the door slightly opening and pincher pokes her head around and asks me if I want breakfast. "I have Irish bacon and sausages and black and white pudding," she says, smiling. "That would be great; I'm starving. Thanks." I'm thinking to myself that breakfast in bed would be nice, and then maybe a shag. I suppose that would be pushing it. I just don't want to leave this bed. There's nothing better after a feed of drink than a greasy Irish breakfast—well, almost nothing. I start to put my clothes on, which were nicely folded on this very expensive-looking chair. I know I didn't do that. I normally wake up and my shoes are still attached to my trousers. The chair is adorned with gold and silver gilt and flowers printed on the cushions. I put my pale Irish arse on it as I put my trousers on—desecrating it, I'm sure. I finish putting on my gear and slide back the curtain to reveal Central Park. Fuckin' Central Park. I'm on Fifth Avenue. One of the most desirable addresses in the world, and I don't even know how I got here.

I leave the bedroom and walk down this long hallway toward where I hear voices. This place is gorgeous. Expensive pieces of art every few steps. This man is making breakfast and there are about four people sitting around a table that probably holds twelve. I sit down and it seems like everybody is looking at me. Actually, everybody was looking at me. *Fuck*, I say to myself as my stomach turns. "Coffee?" "Oh, cheers, that would be great, mate," I say. The dude making breakfast comes over and fills up my cup. Then he says to my girlfriend sitting at the table, "More coffee, honey?" as he kisses her on the top of her head while looking right at me. *What the fuck is going on here?* I think to myself.

Three of the people get up from the table and go into another room. I nod my head as they leave without saying a word.

"Sorry, luv," I whisper, "but your name has slipped my mind."

"It's Abby." "Ah, ya, nice to meet you again. Sorry about last night. I hope I wasn't too much trouble." "Hello, I'm Henry. Nice to meet you," the man says as he hands me my breakfast. "Good to meet ya, man." Leaning over to Abby, I say, "Is this your roommate or something?" "No . . . that's my husband."

"Okay," I say as I lean back into my chair. Kinda *fall* back, to be honest. I put my head down and try to finish my breakfast as quickly as possible. I'm milling it down—sausage, pudding, egg, and piece of toast in my mouth—when Abby says, "I really had a good time last night, hope we can do it again sometime." I nod my head as I force another sausage in my mouth. I'm think-ing if my wife brought some random bartender home one night, I don't think I would be making them breakfast and saying it was nice to meet them. There's something very weird going on here, and I'm not sticking around to find out. Henry sits down between me and Abby and smiles. Awkward silence. Now I'm starting to sweat a little, thinking about all the different scenarios going on here. Like, for instance, where's the bleedin' exit? I know there are people in the other rooms, so I think I'm kinda safe, but I'm holding on to my knife cer-tainly a little tighter than normal. "Listen," I say, "I don't know exactly what's going on here, but I don't want any problems. Sure, I don't even remember half the night. Whatever is going on here, it's not for me. It's not my thing, okay. I'm just going to leave, alright?"

Turns out they are a bunch of swingers who get off when their partners bring strangers home. Also, after I told her that I didn't remember most of the night, she informed me that she had slipped me a mickey. She called it a "muscle relaxer." I call it a mickey (roofie). At least she was honest. Funny, ah.

Well, happy Saint Patrick's Day, Smithy. I hope you had a good one. I cer-tainly had one of the more memorable ones. Cheers, mate.

THIRTY-ONE

Friday, May 23, 2008
New Chapter in America

There's a new chapter in America, but unfortunately it's chapter 11.

I come into work these days and see fewer people—well, the after-work crowd, that is. I come into work at 6 p.m. to start my night; at least I'm supposed to be there at 6 p.m. However, that's a bit of a laugh. Customers actually bet on when I will arrive at work—how many minutes after six I will show up. I hear some cheers and some groans—mostly groans—when I walk in the door, people cursing me for not showing up at their designated time. One customer says to me, "It's not that you're always late; it's just that you never leave on time."

Anyway, don't get me wrong—business is still pretty good at the bar. I'm not complaining. Bars will always be good during hard times; they're recession-proof, I think. People are getting laid off, for sure. Some of them I have always wondered how they had a job in the first place—real fucking gobshits. The others I'm genuinely sorry for, and I wish them all the best.

You hear some interesting things—some funny conversations—while working behind the bar. So many to remember. Here's one I remember from last night:

This guy says to this girl, "What's your zip code?" She's like, "What?" Again he says, "What's your zip code? Everybody asks for the phone number, but I just want the zip code." He was funny; not sure if he ever did get the zip code.

Well, as we all know, times are hard right now, so please, tip your bartender!

Sunday, June 8, 2008
Girls!

As a bartender in NYC, girls are everywhere (like Iggy Pop sings—"Girls, they're all over this world!"). As I said in an earlier letter, bartending is the most fun you can have with your trousers on, sometimes off. I was home the other night with my girlfriend after a long, hard night behind the bar. We went to bed and I fell asleep right away. The next day my girlfriend starts complaining about my stamina—my sexual drive in the sack. So I try to tell her that I was tired and that was all it was, nothing more, nothing less. Well, now I'm getting a bit paranoid, so I asked this older man at the bar for some Viagra. The next night I take six Viagra and wash them down with five cans of Red Bull when I'm leaving the bar to go home to the girlfriend—her funeral is next week!

Speaking about Viagra, I was driving to Upstate New York a while ago to see a friend, and I got to one of those tolls. I'm looking around for some change but can't find any. I reach into my pocket and find a Viagra that one of the customers at the bar gave me. I throw it into the change area, and the toll arm goes straight up. Well, the next day I'm heading back to Manhattan, and I'm going through the same toll and guess what? The toll arm is still up! That shit really works.

Another time I took one and it got stuck in my throat. I had a stiff neck for two weeks. To be honest, I have never taken a Viagra pill—yet—but the commercial really cracks me up. You know, the commercial that says if you have an erection that lasts more than four hours, please consult your doctor immediately. Listen, Smithy, if I have a hard-on that lasts for more than four hours, I'm calling every girl I have ever known!

Talking about erection pills, another fella asked me, "What about Cialis?" I say, "I have enough problems with my own girlfriend. I don't want to see Alice."

Sex—there are many reasons to have sex: the condoms are about to expire, hotel sex, foreigner sex, makeup sex, breakup sex (my personal favorite), new position sex, can't sleep sex, Chinese food sex . . . . Is it me or is Chinese food the best after—or sometimes during—sex food? Just don't get the egg rolls mixed up.

While I'm "expressing" myself, did you ever see how many onion rings you can fit on your penis? You'd better let them cool off first. I made that mistake.

Ever with your girlfriend and you get a quick fart in while she's in the bathroom? Squeeze one out real fast. Oh, what a relief.

I've been using anti-wrinkle creams to look younger, but they don't work. My balls still look all wrinkly and old.

Well, I think that's enough "expressing" myself for now. Good luck and cheers for now, and remember to tip your bartender!

Monday, July 21, 2008
George Michael in the Garden Tonight

Busy night at the bar tonight—busier than a usual Monday night. George Michael was in Madison Square Garden tonight, which is probably why we were busier than normal. It's always busier when there's something going on at the Garden. Apparently still a lot of Wham! and George Michael fans around. By the way, what's white and slides down the bathroom wall? George Michael's latest release. Just kidding, George.

Talking about celebrities, David Hasselhoff was in the bar tonight. You remember him from *Baywatch* or what we liked to call it—*Wank Watch*. Maybe he's a George Michael fan, or maybe he was meeting him in a public toilet afterward. Who knows? Anyway, he comes up to the bar, and I say, "Hello, Mr. Hasselhoff, what can I get you?" He says, "Please, call me . . . Hoff." "Sure, no problem . . . Hoff." Whatever, weirdo. By the end of the night everybody in the bar is calling him Hoff. Hoff this and Hoff that. I was actually getting a bit sick of this, so when he came up to the bar, I said to him, "So why do you want to be called Hoff? What's with all this Hoff bullshit?" He replied, "Listen, I don't want any Hassel . . . ."

THIRTY-TWO

Monday, August 25, 2008
Oh, Not Again!

It's a quiet Monday night as the summer is coming to an end. The last few weeks in August are generally the slowest weeks of the year, as most people are out of town on holiday. I enjoy this time of the year, to be honest. As you know, Smithy, I love the hot weather—so nice and hot. Also the city is dead—quiet and calm.

I'm about to close the bar when this big tall guy walks in, all dressed in leather with a big leather cowboy hat on and dark shades—remember, it's three o'clock in the morning. *Unless it's Bono I have a big fuckin' problem*, I'm saying to myself. *Here we go again.* Well, this man dressed in leather says, "Hello there, are you still open?" A sense of relief comes over me. I can feel he's okay and isn't going to give me any problems. I say, "Sure, why not? You're good for one drink, but I'm closing up soon." He orders a black and tan and a Jager bomb and asks me if I would like one too. Turns out Michael, also known as "black and tan," is quite an interesting guy, and we end up talking for a few more hours. He tells me he's just back from interviewing Les Paul (the inventor of the electric guitar) after his Monday night show at the Iridium Jazz Club in Times Square. We have a great laugh together, and just as he leaves at six o'clock in the morning, he tells me that his friend Brad is coming into town tomorrow and that he will send him in. As he walks out the door, he turns and says, "By the way, Brad is blind."

Sure enough, about eight o'clock the next night, Brad rolls in, cane and all. I make room for him at the bar and he sits down. Totally blind. He introduces himself and asks for a Guinness. What a remarkable man he was, walking around Manhattan totally blind. I can hardly do it with two functional eyes. He tells me he's a professor of history in North Carolina and is in town promoting his book, which is about the Irish and how the bar plays such a role in their lives and community. I think he's in good company. We party together all night, along with most of the bar, and the craic is brilliant. We sing songs (he plays the guitar), and we tell jokes all night until closing time. I walk up the street with him to his hotel on Thirty-Sixth Street between Ninth and Tenth Avenues. Talk about the blind leading the blind. I walk Brad to the entrance of the Comfort Inn and tell him that there are about ten steps down into the hotel and to grab the handrail. He turns around and "looks" at me and says, "Handrails are for pussies," and walks right down the middle of the steps without missing a beat, or more importantly, a step. It's incredible how people can overcome disabilities, and Brad has certainly done that. Now, whenever Brad is in town, he always pops in to "see" me. I couldn't resist, Smithy!

Thursday, September 25, 2008
When You Got to Go, You Got to Go!

On Thursday night a couple of us headed down to this new bar in the village. The bar was as lively and as lawless as any I've ever witnessed. It reminded me of the old days in New York when "anything goes" was the attitude in the bars. It seemed that you could do anything there. The bar staff (who were all gorgeous, by the way) invited us to pour our own drinks as they focused their energies on helping patrons, two at a time, onto a huge podium behind the island bar, to dance or strip, depending on what took their fancy. I explained that I was actually a bartender and that the novelty of making more drinks, however exciting, would be lost on me. My friends, on the other hand, were loving it. Tammy from Tennessee, with her thick full lips and deep probing eyes, then pours me a rather large shot of tequila, and we both say cheers and knock them back. One of the many cool things about being a bartender in New York is the great after-hours. Once they know you're a bartender particularly, you can usually stay as long as the bartender wants to. They know they are going to get a good tip, and they also know that you know how to behave yourself. Party on.

Soon everyone was dancing on tables, bars, and podiums. At an opportune moment the large podium behind the bar cleared, and Tammy and I sensed this was our cue to show off our moves. Well, I sensed it was. We jumped up onto the vacant podium, and I immediately launched into my trademark breakdancing routine. Performing my lame knee and head spins, before finishing off with the custom body wave. Normally this is guaranteed to make any girl run for her life, but not Tammy. She actually thought I was serious, and what's more, she thought I was good. Of all the descriptions of my dancing I ever got in the past, "good" was never one. We were getting along famously, and I soon found myself sharing a taxi back to her place.

The taxi ride took about ten minutes as we arrived on West Forty-Eighth Street, right off the West Side Highway. We entered the cold building and climbed the concrete staircase to the fourth floor. It had been a rough week— drinking a lot—and again I found myself in this strange apartment, drunk.

"Please be careful. Lilly does not like men very much," Tammy informed me as she opened the door. Lilly, I soon discovered, was her Doberman. Why is it that ferocious dogs tend to have pretty names? They should be called what they are: Killer or Rip Your Fuckin' Balls Off—something a little more appropriate. Lilly greeted Tammy with a wagging tail and licking tongue, a display of affection that ended as soon as I walked through the door. Lilly immediately bared her front teeth and growled menacingly. Tammy held Lilly firmly by the collar as I slid with my back along the wall, holding my town halls to get past. After all, I was hoping to use them tonight, or this morning now. She was correct: Lilly didn't seem to like men very much.

"Its okay," she assured me. "Come on, we must walk Lilly."

Was she serious? It was six o'clock in the morning, and she wanted to walk her dog! I was starting to really dislike Lilly, who growled as I shot her an angry glance. We walked back down the four flights of stairs and out into the cold morning. It took Lilly twenty minutes to mark her territory and clear her bowels (I think she was just fucking with me), in what was, without doubt, some of the longest twenty minutes of my life.

Back at the apartment Tammy and I returned to her room and quickly took off a few layers of clothing before jumping into bed. Her room was manky; mind you, messy women are great in the sack, so it was okay with me. As we started to get comfortable with one another, I heard the pitter-patter of feet behind me. I turned around to see Lilly's face, including her shiny teeth, about three inches from my face. She made no noise, but it was clear she didn't approve.

"Don't worry about Lilly. She is just a big teddy bear," soothed Tammy. But I did worry about Lilly. She was a big teddy bear with big, sharp fuckin' teeth.

I wake up in this dark room, not remembering too much and needing to go to the bathroom—quickly. I'm not talking I can hold it in for a few minutes. I mean my arse is going to sneeze any second now. I mean, do farts have lumps? I'm thinking, *Where the fuck is the door in this room?* Everything is pitch-dark; I can't see a fuckin' thing. All I see is the outline of a window. I pull across the curtain to let some light into this dark, disgusting room. It's just a dark alley in between many apartment buildings. It's there and then that I have to go. By the way, I'm not proud of what happened next. I barely get the window open before I launch my arse out it, just as my arse sneezes out the window—should not have had all those pints of Guinness and shots the night before. I'm sitting there with my arse out this stranger's window, relieved and wondering first, *Where the fuck am I?* And second, *How am I going to wipe my arse and get the fuck out of here as quickly as possible?* So what do I do but wipe my arse on these lovely white curtains that are still in my hand. Actually they're not that nice. They were white and pretty, I'm sure, at one time, but they are now a yellow smoky color. Well, they're ruined now. I felt so bad and obviously got out of there as quickly as possible. As I'm leaving I see the dog, now sitting up and growling at me. Fuck, Lilly, right, as some of it starts coming back to me again. *Please don't bark and wake her up. Please don't bark and wake her up,* I repeat to myself. I slip very slowly past the dog. At least Lilly might understand—when you gotta go, you gotta go. I did walk her last night, after all. I went straight home, showered up, and went back to bed. What will happen tonight?

THIRTY-THREE

Saturday, October 18, 2008
"The Great White Way"

My mother is over with me this week. I have planned, hopefully, a good New York City night for us tomorrow. Dinner, Broadway show, and maybe after, a nightcap or two. If I know my mother, she's up for anything. I really relish going to a play on Broadway; there's no place like it. The Great White Way, as the New Yorkers would say. I'm telling a few cop friends about my mother coming over and the night I have lined up for us. They are excited for me, I think, and offer to give us a police escort from the restaurant to the Broadway show. "That would be brilliant, and my mother would get such a kick out of it," I say. They tell me to text them when we are finished with our dinner.

So our big night is upon us, and we head to Uncle Jack's Steakhouse on Ninth Avenue and Thirty-Fourth Street to start it off. We have a lovely dinner, and we are now having a glass of wine with Brian the bartender at the bar. By the way, my mother has no idea about the police escort. As we are sitting there chatting at the bar, I send off a text letting my friends know we are ready. I get a text back right away, saying, "Outside ten minutes." The handy thing about it is, the police station is right around the corner from the restaurant, on Thirty-Fifth. We settle up and make our way out to the front of the restaurant. Sure enough, a police car shows up within seconds. Out jump my two friends, and I say to my mother, "Our ride is here." She thinks I'm joking until they introduce themselves to her and tell us to get in. We're like two excited kids in the back of the car as we buckle up and they say, "You ready? Well, hold on!"

Before we know it, the lights are flashing and we dash across Thirty-Fourth and make a quick right toward the entrance to the Lincoln Tunnel. We veer to the left and head towards Forty-Second Street and make a boisterous right. We are sliding back and forth and left and right in the back of the police car, looking at each other and giggling away. We are now on Forty-Second Street—on the wrong side of the street. Our theater is on the right between Seventh and Eighth Avenues. What a rush as we turn across traffic and stop right outside the New Amsterdam Theater to see "Mary Poppins." We get out, not really comprehending what actually just happened. Only took us about four minutes to get there. If we were in a taxi, we would still be on our way, probably still outside the restaurant. As I'm sure you know, traffic in NYC is a nightmare, especially on a Saturday night. We take some pictures outside the theater with the police officers. My mother is wearing one of their police hats. We thank them, say our goodbyes, and take our seats a couple of rows from the stage, still in shock, laughing away—sniggering like a couple of schoolkids. What a way to travel and a perfect all-round night in the big city.

Out to dinner with Mum, Dolores

My mother hanging with the cops in NYC

Friday, October 31, 2008
Halloween

Great night at the bar last night—all the ghouls and monsters were out for Halloween. This one guy was dressed like a clansman with a big white sheet over him and a pointy hat. I said to him, "Where did you get the costume—at the KKK-Mart?" Then this bunch of gay lads came into the bar. I like the gay community; they tip well, are usually nice and polite, and seem to clean up whatever neighborhood they move into or live in. However, they say it takes a village to raise a family, but not the Village People. They were the gayest lads I have ever seen. They would have embarrassed Liberace. One lad asked me for some fish stew. I told him we didn't have any.

"No," he said. "I want to fist you." Yaks. I learned something new again today, Smithy.

Well, the bar is neighboring Chelsea, the gay capital of New York City—and probably the world.

There's nothing as funny as seeing a grown man walking down Tenth Avenue at 6 a.m. the morning after Halloween dressed like a slut, with high heels and fishnet stockings on, going home by himself. Try to explain that one. It kinda reminded me of the old days.

Happy Halloween, and don't forget to tip your bartender—no candy, please!

Sunday, November 2, 2008
The New York City Marathon

Marathon Weekend in New York City. It's a great day and very inspiring. I heard a Polish man won the race one year and did a lap of honor—now that's a long lap. I love to run as well, and Central Park, where I usually go, is one of the most remarkable and beautiful parks I have ever seen. I think New Yorkers take it for granted and don't realize how amazing it is. Anyway, I went to buy a new pair of running shoes at Foot Locker the other day. When I got home I noticed that there was only one shoelace in the box. I was obviously a little pissed off, but then I read the box and it said "Taiwan"—think about it, Smithy.

I usually go to Columbus Circle at the Southwest corner of Central Park to see the end of the marathon. It's a couple of hundred yards from the finish.

I got the A train from Forty-Second Street and Eighth Avenue right to Fifty-Ninth and Columbus Circle. The subway is the best way to get around in this town.

If you're a tourist, go down to any subway station and ask the person in the booth for a free subway map. Get your bearings and go off and explore this great city—it's that easy . . . except for all the people, the inaudible announcements on the subway trains, and the rude staff, it's all good. That's why it's important to have your map and be prepared, plus there is always a map on the trains and on the platforms.

For the New Yorkers, we all know that the seat underneath the map on the subway is the worst seat on the train, as people are constantly coming up and looking at the map and sticking their dirty, sweaty balls, big tits, or smelly arses in your face while they are figuring out what stop to get off at. By the way, there was a shock at the marathon this year—a Kenyan won it!

Enjoy, and cheers for now. Talk to ya soon, Smithy.

Wednesday, November 19, 2008
Comedian Dane Cook in Madison Square Garden

The bar is busy as people are coming in to warm up from the cold. I am making a lot of hot whiskeys and Irish coffees. On my night off on Sunday, I went to see the comedian Dane Cook in Madison Square Garden. Always thrilling to go to the Garden; as they say, it's the world's most famous arena. Dane Cook was pretty funny, you have to give it to him. He sold out two shows in the one night—just him, no warm-up artists. He said that his dad would always say to him when he was a kid, "Don't try and pull the wool over my eyes; you know I've been around the block," and Dane would say, "That's because you're always too drunk to find the house." I thought that was pretty funny, and it reminded me of my dad. My dad used to say to me, "Did you take your ugly tablets today, son?" That's not a nice thing to say to your son, now, is it? I would say, "Shut up, big ears, I know you can hear me." And you wonder why I ended up the way I did. My dad has big ears, like two satellite dishes, like the FA cup.

Well, after the gig we treated ourselves and headed up to the Oak Room Bar at the Plaza Hotel across from Central Park. It's a wee bit too stuffy for us, but it's nice to rub shoulders with the wealthy New Yorkers once in a while. It's a fancy joint—a place that has bathroom attendants. Are bathroom attendants ever necessary? I don't think so. First of all, they hate you, and you hate them. They make you feel so uncomfortable. It's kinda like when you're in an elevator with a bunch of strangers, but this time you have your penis in your hand. You're hoping you can get in and out of there without any eye contact. They know that, and they fuck with you. Come on, I'm an adult. I don't need anybody to put soap on my hands and dry them for me. Have you ever been to the bathroom and thought, *Fuck, if only I had a mint?*

They said today in the *New York Daily News* that James Hetfield, the lead singer of Metallica, the heavy metal band, was arrested in Kennedy Airport for continually setting off the heavy metal detectors.

There is a new drink in the bar called a Starburst, which is all the flavored Stoli vodkas and cranberry juice in a shot, and we're not finished there. Then you drop it in a half pint of Red Bull. My friend, let's say "Bob," had this drink, and before he knew it, ended up with more Southern hospitality than he expected, grits and all. Ended up going home with a nice Southern lady who was at the bar. A Georgia peach. How do you get two people together who have no reason to be together? Starburst! But did he get the real Southern hospitality? Well, that's for our imagination. Cheers, Bob, and good luck.

Friday, November 28, 2008
Singer Morrissey in Town Tonight

All the Irish and British fans of The Smiths (an Englishman with an Irish heart) will love the return of Morrissey to NYC tonight and through the week at one of New York's hippest and coolest venues, the Manhattan Center (Hammerstein Ballroom). It's always busy when there's a concert, in either the Manhattan Center or in Madison Square Garden.

Great night tonight at the bar—good crowd with little incidents and loads of tips. Sometimes I just don't get people. A bunch of people come into the bar at around 3:45 a.m. and ask me for a round of drinks, and I oblige them, of course; it is my job, after all. A couple of pints of beer and a few shots. They pay by credit card and don't leave me a tip, which is fine by me, honestly!

Some people don't tip me and others give me way too much, so I've learned over the years that it all evens itself out at the end of the day, or for me, the night. Now it's about 4:10 a.m. and the guy who just stiffed me asks me for another round after closing time. You want to stay after 4 a.m. and for me to give you another round of drinks, and you didn't give me a tip? You must be completely fucked in the head. Listen, you're the first to go, arsehole. People want another drink after closing time and you don't tip me. What are you, a complete moron? Seriously, you would have to be. I just don't get people sometimes.

That reminds me, a man comes into the bar with just a head, and he says it's his son who was born without a body. He tells me it's his son's twenty-first birthday, so drinks for everyone. All of a sudden, after he helps his son drink, his body appears, and now his son has a complete body—arms and legs, the whole nine yards. It's a miracle!

So they decide to celebrate and have another drink, but this time it has the opposite effect and his son turns back into just a head again. The arms and legs disappear, and he is once again just a head. I say to him, "You shoulda quit while you were ahead!" Cheers!

Wednesday, January 28, 2009
Hit Me, Baby, One More Time!

Britney Spears was in the Garden tonight—a lot of teenyboppers around. Did you know, Smithy, that she just lost custody of her two young kids? Here's my question: Who got custody of Britney Spears? She's the one who needs real help. God bless you, Britney, and good luck. Quiet night in the bar tonight, but a very eventful ending. I'm walking out of the bar around three thirty in the morning. It's obviously dark, so I'm always looking around when leaving. Out of nowhere this guy comes toward me. I think to myself, *Fuck, this is not good.* As a bartender, you always have a few dollars on you. As he comes toward me he stops about two feet away from me and says, "Do you want a blow job?" I was never so relieved, if you know what I mean. I thought I was about to get robbed again, and this guy says, "Do you want a blow job?" I say, "Nay, not tonight, mate, but maybe another night."

No, I say, "Get the fuck away from me, you sick fucker." Then he says to me next, to sweeten the deal, I suppose, "I will swallow." Like now I was going to say, "Well, now that you're going to swallow, well . . . okay then." You never know who or what's out there in the night in New York City, Smithy. Talk to you soon, buddy.

THIRTY-FOUR

Congratulations to President Barack Obama. I think America is ready for a black president. Well, the last one was retarded, so why not a black president? I voted for President Obama. I like him, and I'm proud I voted for him, but let's be honest: every single black person in America voted for Obama because he's black. Come on. What does he stand for? Fucked if I know; he's black—good enough for me. Can't say I blame them. Like if you were in a pick-up basketball game, I'm picking the black guy every single time, and you can be sure the black guy is. I would vote for the pale, white Irish dude everytime. I wouldn't care what his political views were. He's Irish—oh he's the one for me.

George W. Bush was in the bar last night, looking to get laid—doesn't have much to do these days. He said to this brunette girl at the bar, "I was the president of America. How much would it cost me to spend some time with you?" She replied, "Two hundred dollars." Then he asked this redheaded girl the same question, and her reply was, "One hundred dollars." Lastly he asked this blonde, and she replied, "Mr. President, if you can get my skirt as high as my taxes, my panties as low as my wages, your dick as hard as the times we are living in, keep it rising like the price of gas, and screw me the way you have the American people, then it won't cost you a fucking penny!"

The bar is closed today for President's Day; it's always nice to get an extra day off, so happy President's Day, everybody. God bless all. President George W. Bush said he really loves President's Day, as he always looks forward to all the presents.

President Bush said every illegal immigrant coming to America should learn English, since "if I was moving to Canada, I would learn Canadian." Way to go, George! I am definitely getting audited this year. He was recently in England and had to go into the hospital for an emergency circumcision, but the doctor said he would not be able to do the operation because, as he said, "There is no end to this prick." When having sex, George Bush always has to be on the bottom, as he can only fuck up!

Vice President Dick Cheney said today that if everything goes well with the war in Iraq, there would be three different countries—regular, unleaded, and supreme. Dick Cheney sounds like something Hillary Clinton shoulda had for Bill.

That reminds me of the night Monica Lewinsky came into the bar. I asked her, "Who will you be voting for in the upcoming presidential elections? Will you be voting for Hillary Clinton (don't get ahead of me), Barack Obama, or John McCain?" She said, "I will be voting Republican, as the Democrats left a bad taste in my mouth." So I presume it's John McCain for president then. Thanks, Monica.

I think we should get an Italian president. I know if we had one, the war would be well over by now. In the press conference, a news reporter would ask the president, "So how did you end the war?" The Italian president would say, "Don't worry about it. I sent Vinnie and Joe-Joe over and they, how should I put it, had a little chat. Vinnie showed him his baseball bat and *boom boom*, fuhgeddaboudit."

All good bartenders have jokes, so here's one: President Bush, Pope Benedict, and Michael Jackson are on a plane. It's going down and they only have two parachutes. The crew says to the pope, "We think you should be the first to take a parachute; you need to survive." The pope says, "No, I can't; what about the children aboard the plane?" President Bush says, "Fuck the children," and Michael Jackson says, "Do you think we have time?"

Cheers, Smithy, enjoy President's Day, God bless America, and remember to tip your bartender.

Sunday, March 1, 2009
Conversations Overheard at the Bar

Three doctors are discussing their countries' medical achievements. The German doctor says, "We can take a kidney out of a man and put it in another man, and he will be up and looking for work in six months." The English doctor says, "We can take a lung out of a man and put it in another and he will be up and looking for work in five months." Then an American doctor says, "We can take an arsehole out of Texas and put him in charge of the country and we will all be out of work."

I was in a bar quiz the other night, Smithy, at the Broadway Dive bar on 102nd Street and, you guessed it, Broadway. I lost by one point. The losing question was: Where do women have the curliest hair? Apparently the correct answer was Fiji. Who knew?

I was home last night with my new girlfriend. She's really nice, and I like her a lot. I have the apartment to myself as my roommate is out of town. Candles lit and a nice bottle of wine. Setting the mood for a lovely romantic night. She's on the couch looking all cute and sexy in her jammies and New York Giants T-shirt. I'm in the kitchen making my favorite dish, scallops and mussels in a spicy red sauce. We're enjoying our red wine, really having a grand night.

Dinner is ready, and I bring it into the living room. I place her dinner in front of her and say, "You want to move in?" She jumps up screaming, all excited, "Oh, I would love to move in with you." She's hugging and kissing me. "This will be great; I'm so happy."

"No . . . no, I mean . . . can you move into the middle of the couch so I can sit down beside you?"

This is kinda awkward now, isn't it, Smithy? Fuck, that was an uncomfortable few minutes. I think we need to slow things down a wee bit, ah?

Thursday, May 14, 2009
Give People the Benefit of the Doubt?

Coming from Dublin, Ireland, as you know, Smithy, it's hard to trust people whom you don't know. We're not very trusting, I think. There are a lot of scammers around. Living in America over the last ten years I have learned to give people the benefit of the doubt—even in New York City. This girl from Buffalo, which is in Upstate New York, comes into the bar a few nights ago. She is with a few friends. You can see they haven't spent much time in NYC before, as they are asking a lot of questions about the city and places to go. I tell them about a bunch of local places to go, where you will not meet many tourists and will really experience the true NYC. Well, they come in the next night all excited about the places I sent them to the previous night, full of stories. It's what I love to hear, and it makes me feel good that I might even know this town and that I could make their night, so to speak. The girl orders a bunch of drinks and gives me an American Express Gift Card that has a hundred dollars' credit on it. She is a sweet girl, and I know I can trust her. It's a busy night, so I'm running around making drinks and enjoying it all.

You work your best—you fire on all cylinders—when you're busy. I look up and notice that the girl and her friends from Buffalo are gone. Some friends of mine at the bar say that they had said they would be right back. Never saw them again, Smithy. I run their American Express Gift Card and surprise, surprise, it's worth shite. These lovely people from Buffalo, New York, played me. I couldn't believe it. But when I thought about it, I was okay with it. They will get what they deserve eventually. I would have been more upset by somebody who I expected to scam me. They really played me good, but in a way, they played themselves.

Tuesday, June 16, 2009
Porn Stars

I met this porn star at the bar the other night. She works at Flash Dance strip club on Fifty-Second Street and Broadway. She said to me that she wants to go out with me. I asked her when she was available. She said she was working Tuesday and Wednesday, so she suggested Thursday. I said, "How about Monday?"

My friend Joe is a bit of a sick fucker. He told me the other night that he recently bought a blow-up doll, as he was not having much luck with the ladies. The clerk at the sex shop asked him, "Do you want a Christian or a Muslim doll?" He replied, "What's the difference?" The clerk said, "The Muslim doll blows itself up!"

Joe said that he only blows it up halfway so it makes him feel like he's sleeping with a supermodel—told you he was a sick fucker. He told me that he asked his girlfriend to try the missionary position. His girlfriend asked, "What's the missionary position?" He said, "I stay here and you fuck off to Africa." He said he had sex with a female clown; she twisted his penis into a poodle dog. I think I should quiet after that one. Good luck for now, Smithy.

Friday, September 18, 2009
Jimmy Buffett in the Garden Last Night

Jimmy Buffett was in Madison Square Garden tonight, Smithy. Great night, lots of fun. I never made so many margaritas as I did tonight; those parrot heads sure like their margaritas. On the rocks, straight up, with salt . . . either way they lapped them up. It was worth the hassle, as the tips were great at the end of the night—5 a.m.

They're an older crowd, so they are all pretty well-behaved except for this French lad—what an arrogant little shite. I don't want to pick on the French with the old stereotype, but it seems some of them think they are so above everyone else, and this guy was tiny. "Well, pal," I say to this little French cunt, "no wonder you have never won a war when you name your cities Toulouse." Talk about a Napoleon complex. He was so short that when I asked him for his ID, in the photo you could see his feet. I said to him, "Who was the last woman you were inside—the Statue of Liberty?"

I feel better now. See ya soon, Smithy. Go down to your local watering hole and have yourself a margarita—it's on me.

THIRTY-FIVE

Sunday, January 31, 2010
Another Girlfriend Gone!

So my girlfriend decided about a month ago to go back home to Ireland to finish college. Oh well, have a nice trip. I will miss ya. People grow at a different pace, I suppose. About a week after she left, she called and asked me if I could send her back a dildo, as they are "hard" to find in Galway, Ireland. She must be really missing me—ya right! She told me to send it to her mother's house in Waterford, as she would be back there in a week for a few weeks during her break from college. So the next day I go to the Pink Pussycat on West Fourth Street, in Greenwich Village, and purchase the dildo—that's a whole other story. By the way, if you're ever at the Pink Pussycat on West Fourth Street, stop in to the bar next door—The Four-Faced Liar. It's one of my favorite bars in the West Village.

Well, I buy a big green dildo (I am Irish, after all) and post it off to Waterford, Ireland—a small village on the south end of Ireland, about a hundred miles south of Dublin, as you know. Or, as we say in Ireland, about twenty minutes from Dublin. Isn't it funny, Smithy, that everything in Ireland is twenty minutes from Dublin?

About a week after I send it, I get an amusing call from my ex-girlfriend Helen. She says, "I forgot to tell you that my mother's name is also Helen." I think you can see where this is going. So she says to me, "My mother goes to get the post the other day and notices a box with her name on it sent all the way from America." Her mother says, "Oh, this is nice; it must be from my sister in the Bronx in New York." So what a surprise she got when she opened the box. Helen has told me that her mother has not left her bedroom for two weeks, and her husband couldn't be happier. Now that's a great end to a story, isn't it—when everybody is happy? Well, two out of three is not too bad anyway—poor Helen.

Well, back to the bar, and don't forget to tip your bartender, but please, no dildos!

Saturday, February 6, 2010
Good Advice?

There was this man at the bar last night who told me his wife's not well. He says, "I brought my wife to the doctor's office for a complete examination, and they have narrowed it down to two things they think she might have: either Alzheimer's disease or AIDS." He was obviously very distraught and didn't know what to do. This is when the advice of bartenders is critical.

I say to him, "Here's what you do: when you're going home tonight with your wife, drop her off a few blocks from where you live, and if she makes it home, don't fuck her!"

That reminds me of another similar story. This man brings his wife to the doctor's office. The doctor examines his wife and says that his wife has "Tom Jones-ism." The man is like, "What?" Again the doctor says, "I've examined your wife and she has Tom Jones-ism." So the man says to the doctor, "Is that rare?" "No," the doctor says, "but it's not UNUSUAL . . . ."

He said his wife was an angel. I said, "You're lucky; my wife is still alive."

Talking about good advice, I asked my dad one time, "Is love real?" "No," he said, "but herpes is, so always wear a condom, son." He was right. Like the Kings of Leon song says, "Sex on fire." I assume they're singing about herpes, gonorrhea, or something like that!

Happiness is having a loving, close-knit family in another country.

Cheers for now, Smithy, and remember to tip your bartender!

THIRTY-SIX

Thursday, March 25, 2010
Coyote Ugly

I went home with this girl last night, and this morning I wake up and realize I made a *huge* mistake. You know those first few seconds when you wake up, look beside you, and realize you fucked up good and proper? God knows, I've woken up with many beauties, but I've also woken up with more horrors than Stephen King. The damage has been done, and now I just need to get this bird outta here as quickly as possible. Cleanup mode. God knows, I can be ugly in the morning, but she definitely abused it. The tide wouldn't take her. A favorite of mine would be to just jump up and say, "Fuck it, I'm late," and run out the door, go down to the local diner that's in my building, get the seat in the corner so I can see my front door, have breakfast, read the paper, and peek over every once in a while, waiting for her to leave. But this one seems like trouble.

She starts trying to mess around with me, but I'm just not into it at all. The only thought I have right now is to get her the fuck out. She jumps on top of me, and it feels like she just punctured one of my kidneys and broke a few of my ribs. I can't bloody breathe. "Come on, you know you want it. What's wrong? You were so into it last night. Come on, baby," she says. "I'm sorry, but I have to go. You've gotta go," I say. "Well, to hell with you," and she gets up off me (thank God), puts her "big knickers" on, grabs her clothes, and storms into the bathroom. I'm lying in bed, hoping she will just leave without any more hostility.

Don't get me wrong, unstable women are usually great in the sack—their self-loathing translates into a great, wild shag—but there are always consequences. If you like the sugar, it will eventually hurt you.

It's like putting sunblock on after you got burnt. It's gonna hurt either way. It's just like life—you can be good at one thing and bad at another. It seems to even itself out. You never get away totally unscathed or scot-free.

Sure enough, the bathroom door opens, and as she walks by the bedroom she gives me the finger and shouts, "Fuck you and your small penis," and slams the front door as she leaves. Best part of that sentence being, "as she leaves."

There's no better sound in the world than the sound of the front door closing after a regrettable night like this.

I jump up, rubbing my hands together and saying, "Thank fuck for that," smile to myself, and head into the bathroom. I open the door and the first thing I notice is the smell. Awful, putrid smell—it fuckin' stinks. I was right not to shag that smelly cow this morning. Next thing, I walk toward the toilet and notice a large, steaming, fresh pile of shite on top of my toilet. It's not inside the bowl; it's right on top of the bleedin' lid. She didn't even open the toilet. She just went right on top. Really, she left me a big steamer as a going-away gift. Didn't even wrap it. I start to gag, pull across the shower curtain, and puke into the bathtub. That's just not right, now, come on.

I really bring sophisticated women home with me, don't I, Smithy?

Well, perhaps I can't complain, and maybe I had that coming after the curtain incident?

Tuesday, May 4, 2010
Bubbles, One of My Favorite Customers!

I call him Bubbles because he always orders champagne, looks like Jack Nicholson, is full of life, and is just a cool fucker. Always love to see Johnny Bubbles come into the bar. Bubbles has been coming in the bar a few years now. He comes in later than normal last night and says to me, "I'm celebrating—champagne for everyone." He continues to tell me that he is having a party and would love for me to attend. He's a lawyer and was celebrating, I'm sure, fucking somebody over. He's really one of the good ones. Actually, he says, "You fucking better attend," and with an invitation like that, I head up to Park Avenue around Fiftieth Street after work. I go in what looks like an office building, and I tell the man at the door my name. He says, "Please, sir, go right ahead. He is expecting you." I love Johnny Bubbles.

Well, the elevator opens up and the first thing I see is a group of three naked Asian ladies playing pool (still no sign of Nina). What a bloody surprise. Johnny Bubbles comes out from one of the rooms, smiling from ear to ear. His arms are around two girls, with a glass of champagne in each hand—what else? "Here," he says as he hands me a glass of champagne. "Great to see you outside the bar. Please, enjoy everything." He opens up his arms to show off the whole room, like he's showing off a smorgasbord of delights or something. There's a bar in one corner with a bunch of happy-looking people sitting at it, some very pretty-looking lady's splashing around in a Jacuzzi in the other corner, and people coming and going out of all the various rooms. Then I see that the Asian ladies are not playing pool at all but are actually using the pool table to do cocaine off of it. Like Scarface—what a party. I asked the Asian girls if they knew my friend Nina, as they all know each other, right? Still no luck. Whatever I said about lawyers before, I take it back. They sure know how to party. Well, that's all I can say for now. By the way, did I tell you I love Johnny Bubbles?

THIRTY-SEVEN

Wednesday, May 12, 2010
Drinking Too Much These Days?

When you're a bartender, there always seems to be a reason to drink, not to mention, it's right there, all around you. You're surrounded by it. These days I feel like there is constantly a reason to drink, and now I'm actually starting to believe those reasons. I'm even starting to make up reasons. Reasons like: it's Monday, it's Friday, it's going to be a late one tonight, my friends are in, the girls are in, the cops are in, it will take the edge off, and so on.

This list of reasons or excuses could go on forever. This all catches up with you if you're not careful. After a while the nights start getting longer and the days get shorter. All of a sudden it's just a couple of comatose waking hours during the day before you have to head back to the bar and do it all over again.

I feel like I'm coming close to the line of drinking for fun and to be sociable, as compared to drinking to dull my senses and to just check out of life for a while. I'm hydroplaning over life—feeling like I barely have a smidgen of stability or normalcy in my life. A lot of worrysome thoughts scurry around in my head—like it's a pinball machine. A very pensive atmosphere in there. It feels like it just happened overnight, but in reality it's probably been coming for a while. I've been on a mission of self-destruction for a while now. I pretend to go slow when I want to go fast. I'm getting to a stage where I say to myself, *Fuck it, I'm getting pissed tonight.* It's all or nothing these days. To make it simple, Smithy, I am drinking to get drunk and forget. I wish I had a river sometimes that I could flow away on. It's a slippery slope and a dangerous line to cross, I believe. I have seen many customers at the bar and friends of mine go down that very road.

New York City is actually a great place to hide—if that's what you want to do. You can go from bar to bar and nobody will say a word to you. You could really support alcohol addiction quite easily. It can be a very lonely town—an unforgiving place. You might think with over eight million people that you would have a difficult time hiding, but it's not the case. People really leave you alone. God forbid your neighbors would talk to you. You're lucky if you get a nod in the morning. You can really feel very isolated if you choose to be.

I'm starting to spend too much time by myself. I think it's good and important to spend time alone, for personal growth, to enjoy your own company, but it's equally important that you have other people's company. It's actually essential. From the beginning of time, we have always communicated with others. Right now it's just me. I'm slowly removing myself socially . . . and I'm a bartender in NYC.

It's, right now, almost out of my control. I have those talks with myself all the time—*come on, get a grip*—but I'm too weak and powerless right now. Maybe it just needs to run its course—I'm not sure. Drinking numbs my wits and makes it slightly more bearable.

I think everyone goes through times in their life when they need spiritual help and guidance—maybe this is my time? But you know what, I'm going to be okay. You know why? Because there is no other option, and I have to.

Like my buddy Kurt! We meet up most Saturday afternoons and head to one of our favorite places in the meatpacking district. Tortilla Flats is a great daytime drinking place. You know, before all the yuppies show up. What I've noticed about Kurt recently is how quickly he gets drunk. He's usually pissed after just a few drinks, and I end up bringing him home. He knows it; I can see it in his eyes, and there's nothing he can do about it. It's such a shame because he's a brilliant lad and great to be around when he's sober, or at least up to a couple of drinks. He's just one of those guys who loves life. He reminds me of Kramer from *Seinfeld*. He does anything and says anything without any thought of the consequences. I consider myself quick with a joke but not nearly as sharp as Kurt. He's as swift as they come and is extremely witty.

One time we were walking through Herald Square and he noticed this fella selling sunglasses on the street. He wasn't very busy. Kurt just starts shouting at people passing by, "Who needs sunglasses? Come get your glasses!" The guy sitting behind the table doesn't know what to think. "Whoever buys glasses today gets a free kiss from him," as Kurt points and winks at me. Before we know it, people are crowding around and are actually buying glasses. About an hour and a lot of kisses later, most of his glasses are gone. Kurt's just that kinda guy who wants to help and has fun doing it. When we walked away, I could see that he genuinely felt good about helping the vendor, and he had a huge smile on his face.

But now it's getting to a point that I don't meet him as much anymore. He knows he has a problem with the drink, but ever since his mother died he just seems to not care. I worry about him, and I hope he makes it. I've offered to help him, but until he's ready I really don't know what else to do.

I have actually given up drinking for a while, Smithy, and I don't like it at all. I remember every second of the day since I have not been drinking—I'm bored. I have so much free time. My apartment is spotless, and I'm just waiting for Christmas—I don't like it. I thought the clouds would part, the sun would shine brighter, and I would feel wonderful—I don't. Fuck this, I'm going out for a beer.

There's always another place to go in New York City, particularly in the West Side, Hell's Kitchen area of Manhattan. The West Side of Manhattan seems to be more of the forgotten side of the city. It's more of a working-class area. A "fewer rules" part of the city! A lot more underground clubs and after-hours bars.

Let's go to O'Flaherty's on Forty-Sixth until 8 a.m., then to Smith's on Forty-Fourth and Eighth Avenue, Rudy's on Forty-Fourth and Ninth, or the Holland Bar on Thirty-Ninth and Ninth, all after-hours bars, and then more after-after-hours bars—until it's normal hours again, so to speak. I know that's a lot of *afters*. When one bar closes in New York City, there is always another one opening.

I recently found myself in one of the many hotels in the area with this very intriguing girl I met at the bar. She insisted I come over, so it would have been rude of me not to say yes. I was happy to oblige—right, Smithy? I grabbed a few beers and a bottle of wine for her from the bar and we headed over to her room in the New Yorker Hotel on Thirty-Fourth Street and Eighth Avenue. Well, after about an hour we finish all the beers and the wine, only to attack her minibar. A few hours pass, and the minibar is now completely empty. So "we" have the brilliant idea that I go out and get more beer. I now realize that we didn't come over here to shag, but more importantly to drink—to get drunk.

As I'm walking back through the hallways of the hotel with a six-pack under my arm, starving, I notice a room service tray outside somebody's room. I lift up the top to see a half-eaten turkey club sandwich underneath. I grab the sandwich and start eating it. So now picture this, Smithy: I'm sitting, well, pretty much lying outside a complete stranger's room with a six-pack of beer—actually a four-pack of beer now—eating somebody else's half-eaten turkey club, when it dawns on me, "This turkey club needs mayonnaise . . . ."

Alcohol doesn't make you fat, it makes you lean . . . against tables, floors, chairs, walls, and ugly fuckers, so be careful, my friend.

Alcohol seems to affect women differently from men. Most men, when they go out drinking, don't even remember the name of the bar they were drinking in. Women remember something you did a year ago.

I think you drink in your twenties to get wasted, in your thirties because you're stressed out, and you drink in your forties to forget.

You know you have a drinking problem when the bartender knows your name and you've never been there before. An alcoholic friend of mine is getting married, and he is registered at the local liquor store. He tried the Alcoholics Anonymous twelve-step program, but he fell down the third step—cheers!

I love it when alcoholics say, "I'm doing it one day at a time." That's what we're all doing. Sorry to tell ya, it's called time: sixty seconds a minute, twenty-four hours a day. Can't get away from that.

Tips for drunk people: The next time you fall off a bar stool, pick yourself up "if you can" and say, "I was just trying to break a bar of chocolate in my back pocket." Try it, Smithy.

Remember when we were young, we would pick up some beers (wine for the girls) and walk around the streets of Dublin listening for parties? I was telling somebody this the other night. When we heard people singing, we just had to knock on the door and say that Paddy had sent us. There was always a Paddy—probably why we are called Paddy's. If they'd say, "Where's Paddy?" one of us would reply, "Oh, I just saw him down the road. He was pissed." "Oh, that sounds like him. Come on in, lads." Wasn't that an innocent time?

Where else but in Ireland could you be skint and still get a drink? The best one was when we would look in the newspaper to see who had died. Stop by, pay your respects, and you could drink for free for the rest of the night. By the way, why is it that people always die in alphabetical order?

Do ya remember when we showed up to that house pissed that night? We were so drunk that instead of kneeling at the coffin, we knelt down at the piano. I said to you, "Dead and all that he is, he had a great set of teeth," and you said, "Ya, but he had a bad one here and there."

We eventually got to the body to pay our respects. He had actually died in Spain, and they had to fly him back to Dublin. I remember commenting on the fact that he was a lovely corpse. He looked lovely. A real nice corpse. Those two weeks in Spain did him a world of good!

The body was actually on the kitchen table. They were complaining that they had no room on the table for the refreshments because the body was on it. I suggested that they put a chair under his head, under his arse, and under his legs. They thought it was a great idea, so they shouted up the stairs, "Can we have three chairs for the corpse?" Everyone shouted back, "Hip hip hooray, hip hip hooray, hip hip hooray!" Oh, the good old days.

Until next time, Smithy, and please don't forget to tip your bartender.

Wednesday, June 16, 2010
More Funny Things Heard Behind the Bar

Many people who are ending relationships use this phrase: moving on. They usually say, "I found Steve in bed with my roommate, so I'm moving on." I think to myself, *Actually, Steve sounds like the one who's moving on.*

Or they might say, "I'm leaving Peter. He beat me up yesterday in Central Park. He struck me in the head repeatedly with a pigeon." Occasionally, I get impatient with these people. When they tell me they're moving on, I look at my watch and say, "Well, isn't it about time you got started? No sense in sitting around this bar, talking to me, when you could be out there—moving on."

Favorite word used by women in America: "like." Is it, I wonder, because of Facebook and how everyone wants you to "Like" something? I think they should add a "Hate" button while they're at it. That would weed them out, wouldn't it? How about one step further and go all the way and add a "Fuck off" button? Stop wasting my time and get a life!

Just some ideas, Smithy. Cheers, buddy.

THIRTY-EIGHT

Monday, August 23, 2010
Kurt

It was a beautiful sunny day, not a cloud in the sky, when I got a call: "Kurt died today." It's funny, when the phone rang I already knew. When you die, your eyes are closed but your heart is open. What can I say about Kurt that I haven't already said before? I miss him. He was clearly looking outside for help. I'm sorry I couldn't have done more. There aren't many days that go by that I don't think about him—our Saturday afternoons drinking in Tortilla Flats, our trip to the Bahamas, great conversations, driving home in a taxi with him because he fell on somebody or pissed somebody off, going up to women and asking if he could feel their tits . . . you get the scenarios, right? When I went out with Kurt lately, I always kept one eye on him waiting for his switch to turn to "messy." He was on a different planet. A brilliant, generous person, and one of the funniest fellas I've ever met.

I loved this lad. I certainly didn't love his drunken behavior—but I could understand it. I think we all have somebody in our lives like that. We all might even have a Kurt inside of us. I hope, anyway.

By the way, Smithy, did I ever tell you about our trip to the Bahamas?

Kurt, Hughie, and I decide after a night of heavy drinking to go to the Bahamas. The Bahamas is perfect and only a short two-and-a-half-hour flight from New York City. Kurt works in the building management business and was very successful at it. I would meet him in his office from time to time and then we would go out for lunch. There are a lot of Jewish people in this business, and he always seemed to mess around with them—slag them off, so to speak. As I would get off the phone with him before meeting him at his office, he would say, "Don't forget to bring the pork chops, ya prick." It was harmless fun, but I think he definitely had a love-hate relationship with them.

We all meet for breakfast before we go to the airport. As a joke, I get a yarmulke from my Jewish friend Artie and wear it to breakfast. Kurt says, "You're not fucking Jewish," and we all start laughing. He had a great laugh—a smoker's laugh . . . a laugh that had stories.

We're checking in at the airport, and Kurt is now wearing the yarmulke and asking the Delta agent if she's a good Christian lady and if not, telling her we have room for her, pointing at his yarmulke. He wasn't trying to be mean or anything; there was no anger involved—he was just having fun.

We get on the plane and start drinking right away—it's 10 a.m. There is a "real" Jewish man sitting behind us, and right away Kurt is high-fiving him, asking him where he got his yarmulke. He's well aware Kurt's no Jew. Two rounds in, Kurt is now walking up and down the aisle welcoming everyone on the flight saying, "Don't worry, folks, everything is going to be okay; there's a Jew on board."

We ask for another round, and the stewardess informs us that we are cut off. Kurt says, "Is it because I'm Jewish?" I look around to the Jewish man behind us, and to his credit he is actually laughing. I suppose we are all on our way down to a beautiful tropical island, so it's hard not to be in good form. Well, before we know it, we are served another round. Within minutes Kurt is asleep with his yarmulke now resting over his eyes to keep the sunlight out.

We spent three days in the Bahamas, and we all had a ball.

Kurt was a fuckin' genius. His glitch was his power. His weakness was also his strength. He was that person in class who's already finished the test when most of us are still reading the instructions. Finished first in his class at NYU business school. He laughed in sentences, drank hefty swigs, loved the Cincinnati Reds, and smoked Camels. He always played Coltrane and Van Morrison on the jukebox. We loved him because he was flawed, and his faults were there for everybody to see. Most of us hide our faults and shortcomings; I know I do. Not Kurt—he didn't give a fuck. Every time I see a homeless person, I think of Kurt. Kurt wasn't homeless, don't get me wrong; he just ended up homeless most nights. Come to think about it, there were not too many times when I didn't see him asleep on the street between Thirty-Fourth and Forty-Second Streets, sleeping on his *New York Times*. He was real and was not afraid to be himself. Most of us are afraid to be ourselves—he was not.

There was something totally real about him. We are all so close to being like Kurt—trust me, I'm a bartender. I'm close to being like Kurt.

I saw Kurt just a few weeks ago, and he looked terrible. What happened was, he fell asleep smoking in his apartment, and it started a fire.

He fell over and cracked his head open and lost his short-term memory. I saw him the next day, and he didn't remember seeing me, but I knew he was "in there" somewhere. I could see it in his eyes. At the end, his demeanor and personality resembled more that of his easygoing and loving mother than his more hard, unloving, and severe father. And then, perhaps strangely, he said to me, "I love you."

Maybe he knew.

So two weeks later, I get a call from his family to tell me he had a stroke. (He was forty-two.) I miss you, brother—ya prick. That was one of his favorite things to say. "Ya prick." See you next door.

People with flaws were attracted to him. He was like the spokesperson for drunks, flawed individuals, and brilliant, generous, spirited, wonderful human beings. I wish I had done more for him. For a long time after he died, I felt like this. Could I have done more? After some sleepless nights, he let me go, and I realized there was nothing I could have done; he was going to do it his way after all. He always did.

Kurt

THIRTY-NINE

Monday, January 10, 2011
Technology

I'm sitting on the A train last night heading uptown. I count nine people on the subway carriage that I'm in. Every one of them is on their phone. The lad to my left is playing some kind of a video game, and the woman to my right is watching a video. I assume the rest of them are doing something similar on their phones. The art of conversation is lost, Smithy. Remember when people used to talk to each other, whether they were sitting on the train, bus, or just on the street? Maybe I'm getting old, but I believe eventually nobody will be able to talk to each other if this trend continues. I see people come into my bar, and when the conversation breaks down, right away they reach for their phones. It's like a crutch. At times there are couples at the bar and both of them are texting at the same time. I usually say, "Are you texting each other?"

Eventually we will just text each other and not talk. They will text their drink order to the bar. Social media is preventing people from interacting with one another. People are constantly updating their Facebook status or "checking in." Who gives a bollox? What makes you think I give a fuck that you are sitting in a café in Midtown? Facebook is for lonely people who want to talk to people. I know when I was younger it was fun and a lot easier to talk and get to know people. God forbid you now talk to a complete stranger. It's unheard of these days—it's such a shame. It's what we were founded on—meeting people, getting to know your neighbor, getting along, socializing. Ever watch older people? See how they operate? They seem annoying, don't they, actually talking to people, but in reality they are right. We have gotten so closed off from talking and connecting with people. Old people are just doing what we all used to do. Remember when you used to know everybody's number? Now we don't even know our own numbers. We're getting dumber, it seems.

A friend of mine texted me that he was in a coffee shop. I sent him back a message: "Who gives a fuck?" We're not fuckin' spies or something. Stop sending stupid messages and wasting people's time, for fuck's sake.

Let's all go out and talk to a stranger today. Start at my bar and see how you get on; you might be surprised and even make a friend. Just a thought, Smithy.

Wednesday, May 25, 2011
Stereotypes and Political Correctness!

First, stereotypes. Are stereotypes true? You bet your arse, they are. I'm Irish, and let's be honest, the Irish have a reputation for being drunks and fighters. That is "absolutely correct." I have been a bartender for over ten years in New York City, as you know. The Irish can definitely be drunks. However, I know lots of Irish people who don't drink, but believe me, the ones who do drink certainly make up for the ones who don't. Most of the bar fights I have broken up have involved drunk Irish guys. All stereotypes are true.

Asians are smart, and they like to play cards—that is also true. All the Asian people I know are either accountants or work on Wall Street. We have a Texas Hold'em game at the bar once a week—full of Asians.

Black people don't tip, like fried chicken, and are always late. That is also true. I say that because I'm a bartender and I don't get tips from black people, nor do the waitresses at the bar. Also, we have two black lads who work in the kitchen—they are always late. Why are black people so busy? They're always saying, "I ain't got time for this!" Now come on, that's funny. If it's funny, it's not racist!

The Jews run the banks, law firms, and Hollywood. Just ask my bank manager, Art Goldberg; my lawyers, Jacoby and Meyers; or Steven Spielberg. I wish I were Jewish. They even have wealth in their names: Barry Silver, Nathan Goldberg. The Irish have alcohol in theirs: Paul McGuinness and John Jameson are two friends of ours from Ireland, right, Smithy? They are both drop-dead drunks.

Not all Italians are in the Mafia—but some of them pretend or think they are.

Working behind this bar, I have been lucky enough to meet a lot of people from around the world—people from all different walks of life and ethnicities. New York City is the only place where you could meet someone from Cambodia, Nigeria, and Australia all in the same night. We laugh about stereotypes all the time at the bar. We try and come up with jokes about certain races and ethnicities. Our rule is simple: if it's funny, it's okay. For instance, not all Polish people are obviously stupid; however, there are a lot of dumb jokes targeted toward them—just like blonde jokes. Did you hear about the Polish guy who went to the car show? He spent the whole day looking around the parking lot. What about the Polish man who fell asleep in a microwave? He said he got ten hours' sleep in two minutes! I met this Polish man at the bar one night, and I noticed he had a bandage on each ear. I asked him what happened to his ears. He said, "I was ironing and the phone rang." "But what happened to your other ear?" I asked. He said, "I had to call him back."

Again, this is just a percentage. I'm not saying every Irish guy is a drunk and likes to fight, or that every Asian guy is smart, or that every black guy is cheap and always late. But you can't argue with the percentages. Let's not run away from this—so what, it's okay. Political correctness is getting way out of control; it's got to stop. If somebody makes a comment or tells me a joke about a drunk Irish guy, if it's funny, I laugh; if it's not, I don't. I don't get upset about it, and I would love for the rest of the world to do the same. It would be a funnier world to live in if everybody did. God knows we need it.

The mayor of NYC, Mayor Bloomberg, recently made a comment about how the Irish like to party. It was just a harmless comment. It was not meant to be malicious in any way. This is coming from a highly educated billionaire. (However, that doesn't necessarily mean you're smart—just listen to Donald Trump!) There's a reason why jokes start, and a reason they come from where they come from, because there's an area of truth to them all—that's why they're FUNNY. If somebody told me a joke that started out . . . *Did you hear about the drunk Asian* (well, maybe that's a bad example), I will tell you one thing—it's probably not going to be funny. If the joke started out saying . . . *Did you hear about the drunk Irishman*—it will probably be funny. If an Irish guy, a black guy, a Jewish guy, and an Asian guy walked into a room and in the corner on a table you had a pint of Guinness, a piece of fried chicken, a suitcase full of money, and a calculator, we all know who would grab what. Mind you, the black guy would be late. Let it go, everybody—as my dad always says, "It's only a joke."

Next: political correctness.

Political correctness cripples discourse, creates ugly language, and is generally wrong—it's just not funny anymore. I hear this shite all the time in America. Here are a few examples, Smithy: Remember the lad in our class in Ireland who was as thick as a brick? In America they would be "developmentally disadvantaged" or "learning disabled." No, they're fuckin' stupid. What's wrong with calling them what they are? I think by sugarcoating the facts it only makes it worse.

"The kid's slow"—what happened to this old, reliable explanation? Is it so bad? Really? "The kid is slow." Some kids are quick; they think quickly. Not this kid. "He's slow." It seems humane enough to me. But no. He's "minimally exceptional."

How would you like to be told that about your child? "Oh, Joey's minimally exceptional." Thank God for that! We thought he was just kind of, I don't know, slow or fuckin' stupid. But minimally exceptional! Wow! Wait until I tell our friends.

We hear this a lot in America as well: "undocumented workers." No, they're fucking illegal!

Then, Smithy, there are those who don't quite measure up to society's accepted standards of physical attractiveness. You know, the so-called ugly ones. You can't be "ugly" anymore—you are now "plain." "Oh, look at Susie, isn't she so cute and plain?" No, she's fuckin' ugly. Looks ugly to me. She has a face like a bag of nails. As my good friend Doreen told me at the bar one night: "U.G.L.Y. You ain't got no alibi, you're ugly, you're ugly."

What about the handicapped? They are now "physically challenged." The ones I know hate this word. They prefer "handicapped." I would normally feel sympathy for these people, but the first thing they tell you is that they don't want sympathy—so fuck off.

First of all, the blue parking spaces. That's a great idea. I think most people would agree, those spaces are dead handy—pun intended. I believe it's where the word came from. (You know, Smithy, a lot of people don't know that.) Anyway, these spaces are always near the entrance to the building, and I find that I can get in and out with little or no delay.

Another handicapped feature I really enjoy are the large bathrooms. There's so much room in there to stretch out. I usually work out in them, or sometimes, if I'm out for a while and I know I will get hungry, I will bring a blanket and some food and have myself a wee picnic. I find that once you're locked in there, you can pretty much do whatever you want. One time I had a few friends over and we played cards all night.

And by the way, if there are any stupid, ugly, handicapped people reading this, I'm not talking about you, all right? I'm talking about the *other* stupid, ugly, handicapped people—the ones who'll never see or be able to read this book. Calm down. I'm on your side.

Sunday, October 16, 2011
Shite People Tell Me at the Bar

Vanna White—you know, from the television game show *Wheel of Fortune*—came into the bar the other night. She's a very pretty, striking lady, but whatever you do, don't ask her about her show. I suppose she must get sick of the same stupid questions; God knows I do. Anyway, I asked her what her favorite letters were and she said *F* and *U*, or *FU*. How about that?

It has been a very busy week, Smithy. Comic-Con was on in the Jacob Javits Convention Center. It's a yearly show for comic book fans. It's actually very funny seeing people (adults) walking around NYC and also coming into the bar dressed up in their favorite superhero costumes. The one week out of the year that they take their lips off a loaded shotgun and come out of their dark bedrooms in their parents' basements.

As you know, I'm a bartender in Midtown, Manhattan. Why do people tell me things that they think I might be remotely interested in? They tell me the most painful loads of crap. How dare they think I could be interested in this shite? You know, I can't get those ten minutes of my life back. Hey, mister, I don't give a fuck about your kid's piano lessons. We all love a good story, but most of it is a load of crap, so tell it to someone who cares. Here's a quarter—call someone who cares. I'm like a doctor; I should charge these fuckers by the minute. I was in the bathroom at the urinal, and this drunken man comes in and starts talking to me and then puts his hand around me. My rule in the toilet is simple: don't touch me when I'm touching me. That's simple, right?

One night I'm working—it's a slow night—and I notice this guy walks into the bathroom, and after about a half an hour I see he hasn't came out yet. I walk into the bathroom, and he's just standing there. I say to him, "Are you okay? What are you doing?" He says, "I'm waiting for an employee to wash my hands," as he points to the sign on the wall: EMPLOYEES MUST WASH HANDS.

Do I have to say anything else? I don't think so, Smithy.

Thursday, December 15, 2011
Christmas and the Holidays

The holiday season is warming up, unlike the weather. All the drunks are start-ing to come out. You know it's always the same every year, people going to holiday work parties and drinking more than they should. For the most part, the holiday season is fun and profitable—lots of tips—but what also comes with that is the potential for more drunken pricks. As the crowds grow, so does the chance for trouble, so we all have to be on our toes. Let's hope it's a trouble-free Christmas season. What sometimes happens is, people who nor-mally drink a beer decide because it's a free bar and the boss is picking up the check, they will start drinking double brandies. If you normally drink a beer, do us all a favor and drink a beer and not a double brandy, you greedy fuck. You will thank me later.

I bought my girlfriend two things for Christmas this year, Smithy: a pair of slippers and a vibrator. She said to me, "Why did you buy me two gifts?" I said, "Well, if you don't like the slippers, you can go fuck yourself." I bought her a chair for Christmas last year, but she would not plug it in!

Why can't you say "Merry Christmas" anymore? I said to a customer at the bar, "Merry Christmas," and he said, "It's actually Happy Holidays." When did this happen? I must have missed it. When is this political correctness shite going to stop? It's Merry Fuckin' Christmas, right?

Are they going to change all the Christmas songs, like the classic Bing Crosby Christmas song, "We Wish You a Merry Christmas," or the Bruce Springsteen song, "Merry Christmas, Baby," to "We Wish You a Happy Holi-day," and "Happy Holidays, Baby"? What's next?

I love Christmas; I think there's no place like New York City, especially at Christmas. The city is one bright light, the stores are all decked out, and there is music and carolers everywhere.

The Rockefeller Christmas tree, the soldiers atop the marquee at Radio City Music Hall, and the skating at the Wollman Rink at Central Park—oh, Christmas. The climate settling in and the city bracing for three months of harsh weather marching toward Saint Paddy's.

I remember growing up watching New York movies like *Ghostbusters*, *Taxi Driver*, and Woody Allen's *Manhattan*, as well as the classic Christmas movie *Miracle on Thirty-Fourth Street*, thinking one day I want to live in NYC, and here I am. I know it all sounds lame, but I don't care. By the way, do you know how to make a snow angel? You kill a snowman.

I remember saying to my mother one Christmas, "Don't buy me the bicycle I wanted for Christmas, since I found one in the back of the closet."

Another time I said to my dad that I had my eye on a bicycle for Christmas. He said, "Keep your eye on it, son, because you will never get your arse on it." Now that's just rude, am I right, Smithy?

This lady came up to me at the bar and asked me if I would kiss her under the mistletoe. I said, "I wouldn't kiss you under an anesthetic." Sometimes you just have to be honest. I must be getting old.

Cheers, Smithy, here's to a great Christmas season. Now get out and buy some gifts and have some eggnog. Be extra generous to your bartender, because it's Christmas!

FORTY-ONE

Sunday, May 13, 2012
Gay Marriage

Well, gay marriage is a hot topic these days. I was actually talking about this with a few of my puff friends (just kidding, lads) at the bar last night. My personal view, and I think you know my feelings on the subject, is that you should be able to marry anybody or anything, except your sister—Alabama, West Virginia, and the West of Ireland. Mind you, feelings are like your sister's breasts: you know where they are, but they're better left unfelt. Listen, at the end of the day it's all about the arse you feel beside you—that's it. The arse that you squeeze at the end of the day: male or female, it doesn't matter.

The Catholic Church has some balls (that's just way too easy) to say that gay marriage is wrong and immoral. Talk about the chalice calling the kettle black.

I actually think it should be compulsory for gay people to marry, if you are in an honest and committed relationship. I am actually sick of how good they look, all buffed up and tanned, parading up and down the street all day and night. Let's see how well they would look if they were allowed to get married!

It would be nice to say something to another man and for him to hear and translate exactly what you said—unlike women, who for some reason hear something completely different!

I said to my girlfriend today, "You are so beautiful, darling. You look amazing." She said, "So you think I'm fat, do you?" Now, is it just me, but I have said that to myself a bunch of times and I don't hear or see fat anywhere!

Talking about same-sex marriage, I've been having the same sex for years.

Actually, sometimes people think I'm gay because I'm slim and neat, my apartment is tidy, I'm not married, and I like Tom Cruise just a wee bit too much. Even my boyfriend thinks so!

If my girlfriend ever came home and said she slept with Tom Cruise, I would be like, "Give me details, girlfriend!"

I reckon a lot of gay men stay in the closet because they're so interested in fashion?

By the way, every husband or boyfriend has heard some version of this question: Does this dress make me look fat? Does it make my arse look fat? Every man who lives with a woman has had to sit in that hot seat—in the bathroom, bedroom, hallway, living room, hotel room, pretty much anywhere. They go through an endless parade of outfits—like your very own fashion show—each after the other apparently makes her arse look fat. No matter what kind of man you are, you can *never* utter those words or tell the truth in this situation. Words like, "its fine, luv," "well maybe a wee bit," or "sweetheart, I love the way your arse looks in that, but can we please hurry up?"—those words will get you into a lot of trouble. Lots of nights on the couch. You can never rush a woman when she is trying on clothes! I have spent many years in this situation and have decided to give into this exercise and to just go with it, and she will be ready when she's ready; it's healthier that way. I say to myself, *Relax. Just relax. It's this really hot chick trying on all different outfits. You get to see a sexy girl naked. Just sit back and enjoy the show.* She tries on an outfit, takes it off, then she struts around in her bra and panties looking for another outfit. She takes that off and then her bra. Now she is topless—holy shit. Then she puts high heels on, wearing nothing—fuck, this is hot. When I was a teenager, a hot chick sauntering around your bedroom was considered an impossible event, and here it is happening multiple times a week for free. I'm telling you, Smithy—once you use my system and go with it (because you will never win if you go against it), it just doesn't get any better than this.

What I do now is get changed real quick, run into the kitchen, and stuff some kind of food in my mouth, then lie back on the bed, put my hands behind my head, and just relax and let the games begin. "I don't think that's the right outfit, sweetheart." "I like the dress but without the panties." It turns being late for dinner into an entirely different thing. Just let it go and go with it. Try it, Smithy. It works, and it's a lot of fun.

By the way, Happy Mother's Day to all the beautiful mothers out there. I know many fathers think they should have their own day. Really, all they did was cum—that's it. Fuck off. The women are the real heroes—the real deal. They grow the future, and they are the future. They're perfect—a work of art. You know God took his time, or maybe it was Michelangelo—whoever designed women. All the curves, the breasts and vagina . . . oh so perfect. If I had breasts and a vagina, I would never leave the house.

However, why do women get all the nice names? Vagina and breasts? We get the ugly names: penis and scrotum.

I would go to Vagina and Breasts in a heartbeat on my holidays. They sound warm, friendly, and beautiful—like some tropical island somewhere, surrounded by perfect turquoise water and pristine sandy beaches.

I wouldn't fancy going to Penis or Scrotum. They sound like cold, unpleasant, dull places where it rains all the time—just a thought.

Also, do you ever notice all these women's books and magazines on how to please your man? A hundred and one ways to please your man. Give me a break; stop wasting your money, girls. There are four ways to please your man: give him a good blow job, play with his balls a wee bit, make him a sandwich, and talk less—it's that simple.

That's all I have to say on the topic right now, Smithy, so go out, have a drink, and tip your bartender.

FORTY-TWO

Monday, September 3, 2012
Back in NYC

Just back from Ireland, as you know. Had a great time. Thanks a million, Smithy. It was very strange sleeping in the room that I grew up in, again. The room was tiny; I don't know how my four brothers and I ever fit. There was barely enough room for myself. Anyway, it was a lot of fun to see you and the lads again.

Even though the economy is in the shitter, Ireland is always great craic. I remember a few years ago when everything was hunky-dory in Ireland, the olde "Celtic Tiger" was roaring, and people were talking about how much their houses were worth. Actually, pretty boring shite, to be honest. I remember when I grew up in Ireland, we talked about (besides stealing and girls) art, literature, and politics, and, of course, football. About Bernard Shaw, Brendan Behan, Michael Collins, Liverpool, and Manchester United. I hate to say this, Smithy—I'm sure it's the same all around the world—but we have become boring.

Maybe this collapse in the world economy is a good thing. Maybe we will realize the important things in life again and not how much our houses are worth. People were buying houses left right and center, expecting the prices to continue to go up and up. As they went up and up, we got greedier and greedier, maybe stupider and stupider, and we lost sight of who we are. I was talking to my ma when I was home, and she was telling me how she got an orange and a pair of gloves for Christmas one year—and she was so happy. Now, my ma was born in the forties, and they were obviously different times, particularly during and after the Second World War, but in other ways they are the same.

I'm not suggesting we go back to giving our kids oranges for presents, but let's think about it. One of my brothers has a room in his house that is just for toys. (Remember, we grew up in a room where three of us slept in the same bed!) Now he has a toy room that would make FAO Schwarz look like a garage sale.

So maybe this economic crisis is what we deserve, and we might become a little less greedy, a little bit more creative, and a wee bit more fun to be around.

It's funny, you can't even bring whiskey back on the plane from Ireland—the bleedin' home of whiskey—but Madonna and Angelina Jolie can bring a child back from Africa every time they go there!

Over the many years I have spent in NYC, Smithy, I have compiled a bunch of places that I really enjoy and are in some ways little secrets and gems of the city. Here are a few of them:

Central Park is one of the most beautiful parks in the world. I like to go to the pond by the Plaza Hotel or watch baseball at Heckscher Ballfields. Then I walk through the park and dip into the many museums on either side of the park. Coffee at Café Amrita on 110th Street at the edge of the park. Then I head west to the best BBQ joint in the city—Dinosaur BBQ on 125th Street. Smoke Jazz Club on Broadway and 106th—very reasonable and where all the best jazz players in NYC perform.

Jimmy's Corner Bar on Forty-Fourth in Times Square is probably the best thing in Times Square. Look for Jimmy the ex-boxer. If he's not behind the bar serving them up, you will be sure to see him in the many famous boxing pictures that are on the wall of the bar.

Rudy's Bar on Ninth Avenue and Forty-Fourth Street—just look for the giant red pig outside. Cheep beer and a deadly jukebox.

Cupcake Café on Ninth Avenue and Fortieth Street—the best coffee in town, not to mention the cupcakes, which are consistently voted some of the best cupcakes in the city. Ask for Mike, the owner.

Scallywags Bar and Restaurant down the street on Thirty-Ninth. Tasty food and great pints—a little gem in Hell's Kitchen.

Take the subway down to West Fourth Street and walk around Washington Square Park, home to New York University. Sit by the fountain in the middle of the square. I love to stop by there at night with my favorite person and listen to the local music.

Grab a pint at the Four-Faced Liar on West Fourth Street. Sit on one of the stools by the window and watch the world go by—great people-watching bar. The Comedy Cellar on MacDougal Street is also great.

The Spotted Pig on West Eleventh Street has the best burgers in the city. (It is owned by Bono and Jay-Z.)

Ear Inn on Spring and Greenwich Streets has a great local atmosphere.

The Staten Island Ferry is free and runs every twenty minutes. Great views of Lower Manhattan and the Statue of Liberty.

Walk over the Brooklyn Bridge and get pizza at Grimaldi's, but be prepared to wait.

Explore the East Village and take in Tompkins Square Park. Stop by the bar 7B (where they filmed *Crocodile Dundee* and *The Verdict*, not to mention the countless *Law & Order* episodes). Saint Mark's Place, East Eighth Street. Grip Dogs on Eighth has good hot dogs, but the best part about it is the secret bar that you enter through the phone booth. (Please don't tell!) St. Dymphna's (across the street)—good pub grub and a great happy hour that lasts all day.

On your way across Eighth, look for the building that Led Zeppelin used on the cover of their *Physical Graffiti* album. (Hint: There's a tattoo parlor called Physical Graffiti in the basement—Avenue A, First Avenue.)

One of my favorite places down in the East Village is The Scratcher Bar on Fifth Street between Second and Third Avenue. Live music most nights, and you gotta love the name: "Scratcher." Last but not least, you have McSorley's Old Ale House two streets up on Seventh Street—one of the oldest and coolest bars in town.

Well, that's my little tour of my New York City—just a few of my favorite places. We will do the live tour the next time you're in town.

FORTY-THREE

Tuesday, November 27, 2012
Last Chapter?

This was supposed to be a short-term gig—work as a bartender for a while, make some money, have fun, and do a lot of traveling and position myself for the next big adventure. Well, that was the plan anyway. New York has a way of holding on to you. Well over ten years has passed, and I'm still a bartender on the lovely West Side of Manhattan, Hell's Kitchen—the Manhattan Riviera. A lot has changed, but so many things are still the same. The neighborhood has definitely improved in so many good ways, however, I feel the NYC edge is on the verge of disappearing. The hookers and gangsters have left my neighborhood, replaced by Disney World. Minnie Mouse just doesn't do it for me—nothing beats Pepsi. I certainly don't miss the gangsters. The cool, local daytime drinking bars and restaurants are closing at alarming rates. Thank God Rudy's is still open. (They own the building.) One of the last great daytime drinking bars. Places like Siberia, Collins Bar, Film Center Café, Manganaro's Deli, Cheyenne Diner, and so on—all closed. The dive bars with the great jukeboxes are a thing of the past, unfortunately, replaced by overpriced bars and restaurants full of pretentious shitheads. Invaded by yuppies. Thank God, my bar is still open. (They also own the building.) The key to stopping the greedy landlords from destroying the city is to *be* the landlord. Buy the building if you can!

Business in my bar is still good, considering our economic times. The same people come through the doors, slaves to their jobs. (Just like myself, I suppose.) Coming in before they take their two-hour bus or train ride from Port Authority or Penn Station, only to come back the next day and repeat it all over again—what an existence. Everybody is living for their 401k and pension—pension this and pension that. By the looks of things there will be nothing left anyway—no 401k or pension. It's when I see these people that I realize things, for me, are not so bad. I live up the street, have a ton of fun behind the bar, have met some incredible people, have made lots of friends, and nobody really bothers me, except for the odd gangster, robber, priest, homosexual, lesbian, midget, cop, and pervert. You know what? Bring it on! Here's to another night behind the bar.

I think the key to success in your job and life is, when you start taking things personally, it's time to move on. Get another one. There's a whole life out there that we don't see because we are too busy working. If you can take a look, grab it with both hands.

The problem in America is not the unemployment or the economy. The problem is, the national anthem is boring and crap. It needs to be revamped. For God's sake, it was written in 1814. It's time for a new one. Maybe the theme from *Seinfeld* and end it with the *Law & Order* dong dong, sung by "The Boss," Bruce Springsteen. When you put on the TV in America all you see are reruns of *Seinfeld* and *Law & Order* anyway. Most people would already know it. The new immigrants could learn it while running over the border. It's just an idea. This is the kinda shite that goes through my head. Sometimes I wake up in the middle of the night all excited because of ideas like this that pop into my head. I know—I'm a headbanger!

Why do we go through all this to live in an overpriced, packed joint like New York City? I remember talking to this girl at the bar one night, and she was telling me, "I can last four more days in NYC, ten if I don't eat dinner." It's bloody freezing cold in the winter. It's Godawful uncomfortably hot in the summer. I ask myself this question all the time: why do people live like this? Why do *I* live like this? Americans think New York is strange.

People here might even tell you to "go fuck yourself" when you ask them for directions.

You know why we live here, Smithy? It's because New York City is the greatest city in the world. It beats them all. I have had the opportunity to travel to many places around the world, to many, many cities. New York City is the greatest city of them all. It's the Eighth Wonder of the World.

This city is like a beehive that you poke with a stick.

It's where everything happens, good and bad. It's being connected (and I'm not talking about the Mob) to the world. It's the great symbol of unity and freedom in the world. Why do you think Bin Laden attacked New York? *FREEDOM.* NYC is impatient to any kind of weakness, and because of this, it makes you stronger. Eight million stories. Half of them will not make it. Tears are not allowed. Turns good girls into bad girls. Turns good boys into dipsos. You have every walk of life here, every culture, creed, and religion in the world. You can come to NYC and find someone like you, if you want, or somebody totally different—that's what I love about NYC.

Where else can you pay four million dollars for a one-bedroom apartment? Where else can you be so paranoid and yet right all the time? Where else can you buy a Rolex for ten dollars? Nowhere.

You can always tell a New Yorker, but you can't tell them very much!

I have met some crazy fuckers behind the bar, as you know, Smithy—from all our letters to each other over the years. I've had more brief, intimate encounters than your average serial killer.

But you know what, Smithy? I would not have it any other way. I would not have had the chance to meet all the wonderful people that I have met. All these people who are now a large part of my life. I wouldn't be who I am today without them.

As odd as it seems, Smithy, New York City is a city of trust. It may take some time, but once trust is established, you can forge lifelong bonds.

America is like a camera. If you know what you're doing, you can take a really good picture. If you don't know what you're doing, you won't.

It doesn't matter what part of the human chain you're on—what part of the work chain. From CEO to the tea lady, you're a human being and are just as much a part of the success of this city and world as anyone. I don't think success should be measured by wealth. I think success should be measured by happiness. If you're happy, you are a success. I've met some great people behind the bar, both happy and sad. I've been sad at times in my life, sometimes for long periods of time. I realize now the importance of friends and family. Sounds simple now. Thanks to my family and friends for bringing success into my life, but more importantly, for bringing happiness. Find the joy in your life.

Oh, and by the way, Smithy, guess who I saw today? Nina!

I asked her where she had been—she said she was a little tied up!

Well, I hope you enjoyed my stories, and as always, don't forget to tip your bartender! CHEERS!

IRISH DICTIONARY

Adam and Eve it: Believe it
Arse: Backside
Bird: Girl
Bleedin'/bloody: Used to express serious emphasis
Bollox: Idiot
Brand new: The best
Brasser: Prostitute
Brickin(g) it: Extremely scared (shitting a brick)
Brutal: Terrible
Clattering: Slapping
Craic: Fun
Deadly: Cool
Dipsos: Drunks
Eejit: Idiot
Fair play: Well done
Fella: Male
Few scoops: Few drinks
Flat: Apartment
Gobshite: Fool
Grand: Fine
Gypping: Cheating
Header: Mad
Jacks: Toilet
Jammy: Lucky
Kip: Dump
Kisser: The mouth
Knickers: Panties
Legged it: Run fast
Manky: Dirty

Mickey: Roofie or penis
Milling: Hurriedly
Mugging: Kissing
Pissed: Drunk
Pissed off: Angry
Scratcher: Bed
Shag: Sex
Skint: Broke
Taking the piss: To tease or mock
Top drawer: The best
Town halls: Balls (testicles)
Twisted: Very drunk
Walter Mitties: Titties (breasts)
Wagon: Ugly female
Wanker: A person you don't like
Well oiled: Drunk

CPSIA information can be obtained
at www.ICGtesting.com
Printed in the USA
LVHW041342220621
690840LV00003B/346